THE
POWER
OF DREAMS

The Power of Dreams

First Edition
© Harris Momodu
ISBN: 978-1-916544-02-4

All rights reserved. No part of this publication may be reproduced or transmitted in any form or by any means, electronic or mechanical, including photography, recording, or any information storage or retrieval system without permission in writing from Harris Momodu. The book is sold subject to the condition that it shall not, by way of trade or otherwise, be lent, copied, altered, resold or otherwise circulated without Harris Momodu's prior consent in any form of binding or cover other than that in which is published and without similar a condition, including this condition, being imposed on any subsequent publisher.

Illustrated by Erioluwa Olabode Fadahunsi

Publishing Information
Design & publishing services
provided by JM Agency

www.jm.agency
Kerry, Ireland

THE POWER OF DREAMS

An evolutionary tool for change

HARRIS MOMODU

Contents

Preface	7
Introduction	9
Lucidity	20
Lucidity (Continued)	26
Transform	33
Peace	42
Conflict and Anger	51
Incarnations	60
The Selfish Human Love	64
Suspicious Mind	67
Fear	72
Power of Fear	77
Betrayal, Jealousy and Attachment	85
Guilt	92
The Voyage	96
Receiving Creative Information from Dreams	107
Understanding the Dark Lords	111
Dream and Awake Reality Merge, Change and Trust	116
The Hidden Darkness within Us	122
Anger, Irritation and Worries	126
Generality of Dreams and Spiritual Cleansing Work	133

The Power of the Human Cells	139
Self-Sufficient and Nurtured	153
Two Dreams	157
Lucidity in the True Dream State	162
Conclusion	166
About the Author	170

PREFACE

This book is about using the power of your dreams to become more of the individual you prefer to be. It reveals the ways and provides examples of how to usher in self-development and growth through the landscapes and lessons learned and experienced from dream states.

In *The Power of Dreams*, I describe stories, messages and lessons learned from my dream state, and how I liaised and incorporated them into my real-life experiences and stories.

The world is becoming more aware, more interested, and is looking towards self-development and improvement more keenly now than ever.

Topics like mental health, physical health, and general well-being are being discussed on major mainstream forums around the world. It is indeed a fact that the world needs whatever tools it can get to improve the life of its inhabitants.

As I continued to dive deep into the evolutionary changes in my life, using different tools and information to self-improve move towards and into the type of 'Human Being' I'd like to see myself as, I started to realise that in public gatherings, I mostly attracted the people that were mired in a challenging situation, one that was very similar to what I would have gone through, and from which I emerged with a resolution through my dreams.

I noticed their relief after our conversations. It was as if something in them knew I had somewhat of an answer they could relate to because I had already gone through and experienced whatever they were going through.

Some of them would sometimes say, 'I don't know why I'm even telling you all this.'

I knew I genuinely had something to offer, with the inspiration of putting this book into action so that more from the public can benefit from it.

From all my research into books written on dreams, I could not find one quite like the one I have written, one that looks specifically at self-development and ways to interpret one's own dream. I believe this is a uniqueness that is beneficial for all, as everybody dreams.

INTRODUCTION

Dreams are created from our subconscious and unconscious or superconscious mind[1].

They are simply other realms and realities for us to express our vibratory thoughts, feelings and ideas - the primary essence of creation.

Many scientists, including Albert Einstein and Nikola Tesla, have run numerous tests and experiments to prove the idea that everything in the universe vibrates and has its own unique frequencies. For example, the difference between solid matter and liquid matter is within each unique individual level of vibration, and their individual frequencies.

Oftentimes, lessons can be learned and messages passed on through dreams. As in the idea of having a broader perspective self, Inner self, higher self or spirit self, core consciousness passing on advice to the lower or heavier dimensional, so to speak, physical portions of ourselves, or the identities we believe we are.

---

[1] "The superconscious "also super-conscious or super conscious" is a proposed aspect of mind to accompany the conscious and subconscious and/or unconscious. It is able to acquire knowledge through non-physical or psychic mechanisms and pass that knowledge to the conscious mind". (Source, Wikipedia).

Useful information is transmitted in this way, about how to carry on with the day-to-day creations of our moment to moment reality as we go through our evolutionary stages.

We can also describe dreams as a creative birthplace that can then overflow into the awakened reality.

This can happen in the creation and expression of a so-called bad dream, which can simply be a concept to identify and shed light on the fear energies you still harbor within your vibrational being of existence. To seek and understand the true nature of these fears, so as to deem them irrelevant and no longer serving your true nature, which could be that of pure love and bliss. You can therefore release these fears and allow yourself to transform into higher or lighter states of vibration with peace, love and joy.

In this alignment with a broader perspective, you understand that nothing is really outside of you and no one is really putting this in you or causing this to happen to you. You are not a victim, as it is all within your own creation and doing.

We are all operating within the one unity consciousness. All that is within and outside us is "All that is". So you are everything and responsible for everything that happens to you. I would like to add a saying that everything really *only happens through you*.

There was a time in my life, while I was growing up, when I realized my dreams consisted of whatever ideas or situations I had been thinking of, feeling or experiencing right before I slept. Or they could even be from days or months before this, and the scenarios then expressed in different creative ways for me to explore in my dream states.

This was information that had become lodged or stored within my subconscious mind and began to work and play itself out creatively within my dreams for the purpose of evolutionary growth.

INTRODUCTION

The subconscious mind is like a system of databases that stores programmes of belief systems, ideas and random or not information that has already been worked on or assimilated through a conscious state. This process allows the conscious mind to work on other things and it can then automatically react through the subconscious mind as if playing a programme. The subconscious mind can also be a gateway to the unconscious or superconscious mind (Spirit mind, mind of God), where I believe the life stream flows from. We react innately to gravity, for instance, and our organs continue to function through the subconscious or superconscious mind while we are still asleep.

The mind is split into this duality whereby the conscious mind, 'The masculine,' chooses by generating feelings from the heart, while the subconscious mind, 'The feminine,' has the necessary means to read set feelings and turn whatever has been chosen or felt whether beneficial or not, into reality and it then becomes our true experience.

The subconscious mind is at its peak while we are asleep, so it's a very beneficial practice to consciously choose your feelings and thoughts right before sleep, to get a better benefit of what the subconscious mind will work on for you.

There have been many books written to help people understand more about the meanings of their dreams with explanations of symbols, situations etc.

And many people can give you their perspectives on the meaning of your dreams, which become very useful in forming your own perspective of understanding your dreams.

I for one, due to my own experience over the years exploring my dream state, know that there are many levels to the meaning of a particular dream and that this is due to the multidimensional nature and aspects of dreams. A dream being looked at from different perspectives can have different meanings because of the different levels of understanding. Also, it is not only the dream that is multidimensional, we are all multidimensional beings who can have aspects of ourselves participating at the same time as if we are multitasking within the different levels of the same dream.

For example, let us say that within an overall dream space, there are seven levels of reality and that also we have multitasked aspects of ourselves within the dream, meaning that our consciousness takes part and experiences all the seven levels simultaneously.

While we can retain/remember or bring back relevant information or energies to the awake reality/conscious mind from the first three levels, the other higher levels do not transfer back in the same way, as they are not all that feasible for the awake reality. These higher levels relate to energetically higher activities that the consciousness experiences for the growth of the soul or overall soul collectives or the further expansion of consciousness even though the overall consciousness is already absolute and complete, perfect and expanded. Infinitely and eternally, the vibrations create continuous movements that seemingly mirror and illustrate the illusion of continuous expansion and growth.

Dreams are born on coming out of deep sleep right before waking up. They are just a moment in time, a spark or block of data, which is then stretched out into reality as the stories of experiences within our memories, for more understanding and absorption, which suits the linear and time-based nature of the awake reality matrix we live in. The dream experience in memory also leaves us with resonant feelings or vibrations from living through it.

In deep sleep, there is no time and nothing really exists. Within the inner consciousness or spirit reality, time is multidimensional, meaning a series of moments just like different points or pictures on a negative film strip. Any one point or all points could then be reached simultaneously, while from a linear perspective, the strip is lined up and stretched out step by step, creating linear time. So in a sense, time is an illusion used to create illusions of reality and stories for playfulness, conclusiveness and experience. All illusions are beautiful, wonderful divine dream worlds or game matrices.

Even the awake state reality that we are in now has also been deemed another type of illusionary dream state by those who have had near-death experiences. Some of them have come up with very similar information, such as when they passed on to the spirit state, it felt as if they were just waking up from a very deep sleep and dream state. Now, upon waking up, they feel more like their real self in a much more real reality, with the feeling of joy, peace and unconditional love around them through having this experience and maybe connecting with other loved ones who had already passed on. These experiences are had before coming back to what we call our awake state reality, and some even complain about wanting to go back because they can now really feel the denseness in this "Third density" or so-called awake state physical reality, as the higher realms are much lighter and easier to navigate.

Seeing the dream aspect of our so-called 'awake reality' gives rise to a new extended belief system as there is a way to control aspects of your dream experience through 'Lucidity' and recognising the guidance system within you. When you learn how manifestations happen within dreams, you are able to also control and create what you will 'to a certain degree', within this awake state reality. Hence the popular saying, "*You create your own reality*".

We all have our own unique belief systems that govern how we experience our lives, and we are all entitled to use this however we choose. I must say that my belief systems extend out of the ordinary day to day systems one might come across, so I express a wide range of wild imagination and creation within my dreams and my day to day reality. In this book, I will share some of the stories and explorations of my dreams, with the idea of showing you how I have interpreted, understood and used these dreams to serve me for my further expansion and evolution within my awake state, to achieve more of my heart's desires, which is that of shifting more and more into the unity consciousness of peace, joy, wellness, abundance and unconditional love, through my excitement and the releasing of old energies and belief systems that no longer serve me. The journey I took was to return to the absolute self that I am and that I truly never left, returning back to God, returning to the source, the one within which the dream of consciousness that we all are takes place. Altogether God is the sum of all, everything in existence, nonexistence and beyond. From this perspective, there is no separation and we are all entangled harmoniously in unity as one source.

It is the observatory - a dormant part of consciousness from which the creation and dream of the overall consciousness is derived.

The source, the oneness is the point from which everything contrasts.

And it stays constant so we can experience everything else which changes due to their temporary nature and variability.

That divine illusionary creating state that is in the realm of appearance comes from it without any efforts or actions, while it stays untouched as the necessary void for consciousness and reality to appear within it, emitting an observatory status as awareness. It never started and will never end. It is eternal.

Exploring and knowing the nature of your dreams gives you a better chance to form your own perspectives with the most valid meanings, and you will find out that you are the best analyzer and interpreter of your own dreams once you come to this understanding because it is all happening within you.

INTRODUCTION

This understanding allows you to see and use your dream state as a tool to boost your own evolutionary/growth stages positively, be it communication with spirit "I.e. messages from God", exploration of the superconscious mind within the metaphysics of our reality, playing out a scenario to transcend particular energies within the consciousness or simply just creative ideas that could then be played out and explored within your so-called awake reality state.

Many people have explored and studied the idea of Lucid dreaming. This is a form of dreaming which means simply being awake and aware within a dream state and knowing that it is only a dream. It often comes with the ability to control the dream state, creating at will, with the awareness that you are the creator of the illusion and it can give very deep insights into the nature of dreaming and creating realities. Creating in the awake reality state is also similar to creating in a dream state, with the difference being the dream state is more malleable and easy to navigate than the awake reality state, which is more viscous and tougher to navigate as it is believed to be a very solid and real state.

The dream state, on the other hand, is believed to be an illusion since one is lucid and awake to know that one is in a dream.

The time it takes to see your feelings and thoughts come into manifestation in your very own eyes is much shorter since the density of the dream state is much lighter, so the vibrations move more quickly.

Thoughts

Thoughts are the primary energetic essence needed for creation. We can decide to create a brand new thought that had never been thought before due to new and evolved circumstances, but it may most likely just be a new way of representing thoughts already existing because most thoughts have already been created and are neutrally floating within the ethers or cosmos, to be used by compatible minds.

Once they come in contact with a life node and mind, thoughts become electrically charged neurons like fireflies floating around, and depending on the vibrational mode of the life node, the thought may either remain neutral or become polarised into negative or positive.

If you are in higher and lighter vibrations, if you feel good, you will attract positive thoughts but if you are in lower, heavier and darker vibrations, if you feel bad, you will attract negative thoughts.

A positive thought is like the "1" in binary computer language, the language of "IFÁ" an ancient and Yoruba spiritual method of reading the timelines of life, past, now and future. Also used to read the Akashic records for spiritual messages, this method has been in west Africa for thousands of years before the conceptions of computers or the internet.

It is like reading the waves going in and out within the ocean of life and creation, or should we just say consciousness?

The "1" signifies a positive charge, life and active, a 'Yes' or 'In'. While a negative thought is like the "0" in binary language, which signifies a negative charge, death and inactive, a 'No' or 'Out'.

We are the consciousness in the machine, our physicality, body and mind that receives the thoughts and which then translates to represent and express them, depending on our countenance at the individual moments we are creating.

We can safely say that the thoughts we constantly engage in directly affect the manifestations, quality and type of life we live in. And if we can discipline and still our minds to have more clarity and awareness of what thoughts we harbor, we will realize an empowerment and move towards the best life we want.

This same goes for feelings and emotions because they are tied and intertwined with the thoughts we have. Known thoughts already have feelings assigned to them, which automatically arise as a response to the thoughts, and the subconscious mind, due to previous experience, has already recorded and placed a programme for an automatic agreed response to the said thoughts.

While new thoughts, being neutral at first, will remain neutral until we assign feelings to them based on the maturity of our understanding, and also in response to the situation that brought and attracted them to us.

I will explain the yin and yang duality of this phenomenon furthermore in the following chapters.

Briefly, for now, it consists of masculine and feminine energy, the thought being masculine energy while the feeling is feminine. This duality of energy stems from early parental positions. The father decides on the idea/thought, while the mother has the power/emotions to assign, direct and allow for the outward projections of these thoughts and ideas into physical manifestations. There is always a residual base feeling, frequency or mode emitting from us and this is picked up by a universal law and system of creation called "The law of attraction". This is the divine law that manages all manifestations in the overall system of creation. It aligns like energies with like energies and it is perfect in nature so can never be wrong. Please see excerpts from "Abraham Hicks" for more on this divine law, to realize the universal divine fact that you have the power to consciously create your own reality with your thoughts and feelings.

Because this is what is happening here for everybody, whether they know it consciously or unconsciously and whether they like it or not. Universal laws are almost as if they are written in stone for the set universe and cannot be changed as they are the core and absolute bases of that universe.

I am writing this book, not for the purpose of changing your belief systems, but to provide various aspects of information and understanding that you may resonate with and choose to apply, adapt or get ideas from, for you to better manipulate and create your own day to day experiences.

ONE

LUCIDITY

Early Beginnings of Lucidity

It started when I was eight years old. I had a nightmare of an African masquerade chasing me. The African masquerade is a cultural spiritual display of dances and chants done by humans while all covered up in costumes and peculiar masks. They are seen as mystical beings and feared; they often would carry canes and sticks to chase people, and sometimes you would have to give them money to be free of them. They are widely accepted as a display of culture within Africa.

I woke up on another occasion and the same dream had happened again, the same masquerade with a cane was chasing me. It was indeed a scary dream and because I had now had it twice, I decided to tell my mother about it. She assured me that it was all a dream and, in fact, if it happens again that I should not be afraid. This time I should chase the masquerade back.

I was only about eight years old so I asked her if one could really do that, and she replied, "It is your dream, you can do whatever you like".

I went to sleep and travelled from dream to dream and in the final dream, I had the masquerade chasing me again. I woke up frightened and sweating and realized that I did not remember to chase back as my mother advised. I wondered if this was even a possibility with all the fear I had for such things.

I was determined to do what my mother had advised, I wanted to make her proud because I was her only son and did not want to be seen as a weakling. In Africa, the ancient rule of a man as the head of a house still transpires and a man with no fear is very well respected. From a very young age, she saw me as the man of the house because my father was absent from the home and lived elsewhere.

I dreamt about the masquerade a few times, again and again, always waking up disappointed that because of the fear within me, I was not able to remember what my mother told me and all I did was run for my dear life.

A similar incident happened to me once while I was awake. I then remembered not to go into fear and this gave me much determination, so right before I slept, I was consciously expecting to face this fear in my dream, but this time the dream did not happen.

I did the same thing the next night and I was able to find myself in the dream once again running away from the masquerade, while he kept coming at me with a stick. Then the unbelievable happened. I suddenly remembered what my mother had told me while I was running away to safety. But I found it funny to think of myself chasing after the huge masquerade as I looked back and saw its scary mean face. I murmured to myself saying, "how can this little me, chase this beast away". I was still afraid, so I ran my way back laughing into the awake world.

A very wonderful and quite bizarre feeling overwhelmed me and led to a realisation. The mere fact that I was able to remember what my mother had told me in the awake world while still in the dream had helped me to bridge the gap and connect the existence of both the awake world and the dream world to my conscious mind at the same time. And so put me in a lucid state in the brief moments while running away from the dream in order to wake up.

I explored this feeling for a while. I had just experienced the fact that I was in a dream and could tell it was a dream while still in and experiencing the dream. I thought deeply about what I saw and how I truly felt while running in a lucid state. This was very alien to me at first. It felt very weird and beautifully liberating at the same time. It was quite new to me and very interesting. It really heightened my excitement about dreams in general.

I was so certain that I had discovered something new that I thought was impossible that I tried my best to explain it to whomever I met, adults I trusted and so forth, but no one seemed to be as interested as I would like them to be. I was a little bit disappointed but I went on and also discussed it with my mother, but even she did not give me the response I was looking for. All she said was, "Did you chase it back?" and I said, "No".

I dreamt about it again another night and also entered into a lucid state while I was running and this time, I had enough courage to attempt to stop and look at the masquerade. It looked back at me with a furious energy and was coming after me, this time with full force. I realized I was still not ready so I ran out of the dream to wake up again. I then said to myself as I woke up "I live to fight another day". I was determined to give an answer to my mother that was YES.

This dream happened a couple of more times with me attempting different ways to chase the masquerade back while enjoying all the other aspects of lucidity, gathering information on the different things I could do while being awake in my dreams.

I finally gained enough wisdom, courage and strength to turn back and then realize that the masquerade was no match for me because this was my dream and I could truly do whatever I wanted. So I stopped and looked at the masquerade again, but this time with a strong conviction in my eyes. "I intended to annihilate him".

To my surprise, he realized this very quickly, stopped and stepped backwards slowly. This gave me even more confidence and took me into anger, so this masquerade can be scared of me. He proceeded to run away from me as I angrily chased after it, murmuring again to myself how small the masquerade was. I had allowed myself to be fooled, bothered and afraid and I always had run away. I felt very proud of myself as I saw the masquerade vanishing back into thin air.

I was so delighted while this happened and I found myself floating away as the scenario of the dream changed. It was still in the same environment, a childhood playground where my childhood friends and I embarked on various kinds of games. There was a particular one we called "Police and Thieves" which the setting of the dream had changed into, but it was more like an action movie where real weapons were being used. At first, it looked really real and dangerous as there were bullets and all sorts flying all around. I found myself with the good guys defending and shooting back at the bad guys until I slipped into lucidity again once the threat got stronger. I realized I was in my own dream, and no harm could come to me unless I allowed it to and I could also do whatever I liked as my mother advised. I quickly developed superpowers and started flying around to block all the shots fired towards my crew.

I told them to move back and take cover, that it was my own dream and I could not die, so I took all the shots for them, I was able to defeat the bad guys and I realized I could maneuver better by levitating, floating and flying using my hands to push the air downwards. I realized I was very light and I could really go high and I also learned how to steer right or left. I was even able to use the wind direction, just like an eagle flying from tree to tree or high building to high building and at some point while exploring flight, I woke up.

I was finally able to tell my mother that I had chased the monster back. I then told her everything about the dream and she was quite proud and happy that her son now had a way to resolve nightmares on his own.

I continued to have other lucid dreams exploring this newfound capacity, whereby I would find myself flying and maneuvering amongst many things like spaceships, planes and even other flying beings. It then became a normal way within my dreams to flee away from the sight of things that did not resonate with me.

TWO

LUCIDITY

(Continued)

Dream Memories

'Lucid Dreaming Continued DREAMS WITHIN DREAMS'

As my exploration of lucid dreaming continued, I encountered a very very weird unique experience. It was as if I was waking up and caught up in dreams.

I would wake up from a dream and attempt to go about my daily routine only to realize at some point that this was also another dream, very mind-boggling, right? And this happened about seven times. At some point, I just gave up and said it did not matter anymore if I was still in a dream or finally in the true awake reality.

This is how it all happened, at least from excerpts of the memories I can access at this moment.

We lived in a moderate space 3 bedroom flat on the ground floor of a block of flats. I lived with my four sisters and mother and would sometimes share a room with some of my sisters. Also whenever grandmother 'mama' was around, I would often sleep anywhere that felt comfortable.

I was almost nine years old and sometimes liked to sleep on the couch while watching TV or I would take the cushions from the couch and place them strategically on the floor for maximum relaxation and enjoyment, mostly whenever we were out of light and electricity due to the miss-management of electrical power by the authorities within Nigeria.

As hot as it was in Africa, we grew accustomed to it and found ways to relieve ourselves from the darkness, mosquitoes and heat. I would always look for the best places in the house where the cool breeze could still enter and maybe also have fewer mosquitoes to play with, so I always found somewhere away but not too far from the doors and windows, like the corridor or passageway.

A couple of weeks before the dream, an incident happened. A little fire broke out in the house, which got put out very quickly. I can still remember going to get more water to help the situation.

Unfortunately or fortunately, my favorite couch cushions were affected, but they only got first-degree burns, so they were still very usable and very comfortable for me.

You must be asking, "But how is this all relevant to the experience?" I will say "Memory" is the key word here, because from the memory of the burnt smell, I could pick up more and more images for me to elaborate and give you a greater perspective of my experience. It is as if a vast amount of memory information has been saved within this particular burnt couch smell.

So here I am in the house with no electricity, carrying my favorite couch cushion "now in barbecue flavor" looking for the best spot in the house to spend the night. I decided to lay my beloved cushions in the corridor between the front room and dining room and not too far from the kitchen. I laid on them and tested them and they felt comfortable. I could feel the breeze coming from somewhere so I knew this was the spot. I stood up, went to the kitchen to drink some water and grab hold of some late-night snack, and then went to the bathroom to relieve myself. I washed my hands very thoroughly so as not to fall victim to opportunistic rats that sneak into the houses and could easily take a piece of your finger off if it smelt like food.

This has happened to me before so I was much wiser about it this time. The rats pull this horror off by blowing some sort of cool air while munching on the finger as you sleep, so you do not necessarily feel this when it's happening. Then I finally laid down to have a comfortable night's sleep.

From what I can remember in my dreams, I kept rallying in the kitchen for one of my elder sisters to help me prepare a certain type of meal called "Amala", that I loved so very much, but she kept coming up with a different meal I did not fancy, and as I explored the kitchen to see if I would be able to do this myself, I woke up on the couch cushion which was still smelling so nice and burnt.

I was very glad that it was all a dream because I didn't really know how to cook properly at that time, so I set out to look for my sisters, thinking I was now fully awake and still able to have that meal. I then realized I was not able to find any of my sisters, so I tried going to the kitchen again for a snack but there was none left (*Remember this is now a second level dream state that I have woken up into, but still thinking it was the awake reality*). The solidity within the kitchen changed and quickly became more fluid and elusive, appearing quite difficult for me to grab or hold on to something. Then I woke up again, finding myself on the cushion once again.

I was a bit perplexed and asked myself, "When did I go to sleep again to dream that second dream?", it then became clear to me that I had woken up into another dream and I thought it was the awake state of reality.

So I had a conviction that this third state/realm must be the real deal and I should go and find my sisters once again to complete the quest, but as I stood up and looked around some doubts occurred to me.

However, I continued on. At this point I was still not lucid, it was a perfect dream, and then, of course, it happened again.

I found myself waking up again on my couch and this time, it was not all funny to me. I became completely lucid, very aware but still confused, I did not want to panic as the fear gripped me. In my mind, this had become something else too weird for me to handle, and I was not at all sure what was going on with me.

I could not even get off the couch as I could not tell for sure if this was real or another dream. I thought if I exercised patience, the reality would come and prove itself to me, as opposed to my loitering around trying to get some food because I was still hungry, and then I found out that it was yet another level of the dream that I had now entered into for the fourth time.

Something very interesting happened when I made this choice to wait patiently lying on the cushion. I drifted away from my lucid state on the cushion and went into other little temporary dreams within this fourth level dream state. My memory of what happened here is quite vague but I can still give an account of the type of different beings and worlds I interacted with, most looking otherworldly and some looking like characters from the Cartoon Network channel. Also, toys came alive to play with my friends and me. I can still remember the beautiful, loving, blissful and playful feelings left in me as I left these pockets of short dreams.

When done from these worlds and on my return, I found myself floating back on top of a tree, now heading towards another reality but into the same reality where the couch cushion was. I could see it as I floated through the window, passing through the walls and then automatically merging back into it, and then I got lucid again knowing with no doubt that this was still the fourth level, which I now know is another dream state reality, and I had not truly woken up yet.

I went back into some more explorations of miniature dream realities within this 4th level dream state. On my return back again to the fourth level dream state starting point, I decided that I was done sleeping and exploring the mini dream states.

I attempted to wake up but nothing happened. I got a little scared again and laid back on the couch closing and opening my eyes as if that could stipulate me waking up but nothing seemed to be happening. Then I decided to go back to the kitchen and this time, I found it very interesting as I was fully lucid, knowing all the materials in the kitchen were made from the dream, I saw objects and animals appear as I thought of them - for instance, I saw some ants running around a dirty plate and I then feared that there would be a rat and cockroaches around, and they just appeared as I thought of them. This was becoming more and more interesting as I played with materialization and disappearance, but as I started to have the idea to create my favourite meal, I found myself waking up again, back on the sofa cushions into a fifth level dream state, and this time I was no longer concerned if it was another dream or the awake state reality.

I knew for sure once I started getting back to the cushion from more miniature dreams explorations within this fifth level, at this point I was becoming like a master at this and was greatly enjoying my explorations within these miniature dreams. It was as if I kept going back and forth from a mini dream back to the cushion. There was so much adventure, fantasy and beautiful characters within these mini dreams with much playfulness. And each level of the dream state had its own unique mini worlds to play in, just like different ideas of consciousness.

Once I was finished with all explorations and back within the fifth level dream state couch cushions, I decided to wake myself up again. This time I just thought of food and found myself in a sixth level reality dream state, so I endeavored to enjoy the worlds in between this level too.

In total, I had seven levels of dream states, and once I finally woke up to the awake state reality, it was one of my sisters who came to wake me up and tell me that the food I so longed to eat was ready. I could now tell the distinct difference between this reality and finally, I was able to eat.

This phenomenon of dream experience gave me extensive insight into navigating dreams and it came with an effective way of bringing me into lucidity, which is to be aware and fully awake within a dream, with the luxury of seeing how creation works between a dream, as your internal senses, thoughts and feelings change, the outer environment responds and changes instantly to follow suit.

The senses of smell and hunger were also used as road maps to navigate in and out of the dream state realities. This also helped me, later on in my life, to expand my understanding of timelines and dimensional realities as unique frequencies and also their interconnectedness, where each separate reality is stacked upon each other and one can have sub-layers within a reality. It also enlightened me about our fixed perception of the solidity of matter and the linear timing we operate with within our so-called awake reality, a distinct difference when compared to a dream state reality which is more fluid and can change very easily.

THREE

TRANSFORM

Dream Memories 2013

Transformational Point 1: 'Understanding Clarity'

In 2013, on my way back from Hawaii Maui, where I was for about a week, I slipped into a semi-lucid dream while on the plane.

This was an impromptu trip that I felt I needed very strongly as it was necessary for me to open up more of my heart space and the heart chakra whereby my emotional energetic side is strengthened, for me to better adhere to my inner guidance systems of intuition and heightened sensibility.

Like most people, I grew up with and was taught the survival Philosophy of toughening the heart to survive and protecting myself from the harshness of the outside world. As a man in Africa, it was deemed a weakness to deal with matters of the heart, as this was seen as a feminine trait. But since then, I realized that it was very necessary for the opening of the heart to use and feel the wonderful emotions that guide our creational powers and abilities as humans.

After thirty years of my life and failing to achieve ambitions led by the masculine energy survival ways, I started again from scratch and understood that I had to put a balance between my masculine (mind-based) and feminine (heart-based) energies. I had gone through much research and teachings internally and externally to grasp the importance of this understanding towards my growth, extension and evolution.

From looking at the picture of a very great mountain called the Haleakala mountains in Maui, I felt a great calling of my heart, and reading and learning more about this mountain revealed its association with and transformational powers to help heal and open up the heart space.

It was as if the mountain was saying, 'come to me' and my heart was saying, 'we need to be there'. I literally stood up from my desk at my nine to five day job, shouting to my colleagues and pointing at the screen of my computer with a picture of the mountain, telling them I needed to be there, I then walked up to my boss and asked for a vacation leave immediately, which he approved.

My colleagues were not all that surprised, they just spoke amongst themselves with lots of laughter saying, 'The mad one is at it again'.

After my experience with the mountain, I truly became a changed man. It was on this journey that I found my convictions, and through a series of outstanding phenomena, my heart opened up more and gathered more divine wisdom about unconditional love. I then knew this was going to be my life's journey.

In a dream on my way back, while still sleeping on the plane, I found myself driving my car with my immediate older sister in the passenger seat. Then I sparsely hit another car on the way to some sort of music carnival. The traffic warden got to us screaming and asking if we did not see the car, and then came the owners of the car, they looked like they were coming from the eastern part of Europe.

All of a sudden, there were now hundreds of people and the scenery quickly moved into and around a location that felt like my home. They became very rough and loud and had muddy clothes since they were coming from the outdoor festival, both males and females now looking for some sort of revenge and payback for me hitting one of their cars.

At this point, they carried on vandalizing my car and attempting to destroy some of my property and my musical creations.

At first, I was able to hold my cool and my feelings, and through all this, I remained still and balanced. I strongly believed that no matter what, the situation would eventually resolve itself.

But the heat became more intense as I saw my eldest sister coming out of nowhere, she was not the sister I started with in the dream but here she is, showering blame and guilt on me as I watch these hostile crowds destroying some of my creations.

At this point, a strong negative feeling squeezed out of me and I felt this outstanding anger with a strong knowing that I alone can, in turn, set forth the destruction of these beings in just a second or a fraction of time. This awareness came from my semi-lucid state.

Then it hit me, the turning point realization, instead of taking action or reacting from the anger, I realized that this feeling and knowing of the capability of such a destructive act that I could carry out, made me feel more imprisoned, compared to the unconditional love state of being I had been practicing and would love to continue emulating by going deeper and becoming it, through expressing acceptance and forgiveness. This was indeed the birthplace of utmost freedom.

Quickly I felt that there had to be a common ground harmony and balance to resolve the situation. Due to the openness of my heart and mind, a great idea rushed into my system and I started letting the crowd know that I was one of their beloved artists, musicians they had come to see at the festival. I can even give away some of my materials, as opposed to them destroying what they could find useful.

The entire situation quickly changed with so many apologies and they embraced me as one of their own, carrying me up in the air with delight and praises. I quickly forgave them for being destructive as they realized that they were actually destroying themselves.

After a huge struggle within me, I then realized that I could now let go of these creations that have been destroyed. There would always be more and more new creations to experience and express, as creation is eternal and it never ends.

Back in the awake state of reality, a good while after the dream experience. I found myself in a situation whereby footage of one of my music performances was lost due to a faulty camera.

This really hurt me as I depended on the review of how we did to prepare for the next show. I struggled and could not get over the fact that the footage was just gone like that.

Until somehow, I remembered having similar agony before and then traced it to the dream. Once this connection was made, I immediately felt better and it did not feel that bad anymore. I had gone through this before and was able to let it go due to my realization that creation is eternal and there will always be alternatives.

A few days later, a friend of mine sent us some footage she had taken with her own camera while we were performing. I could not believe my eyes, I was so happy and filled with a lot of gratitude that after everything, I was still able to do my reviews.

I realised that an unfulfilled desire can always be fulfilled, as long as the fact that it is unfulfilled does not affect the dreamer or creator. This fact is accepted and rendered inactive or neutral whereby only the desire remains with the feeling that it will be fulfilled or it is already fulfilled.

Transformational Point 2: 'Lucid Dreaming and the Mountain of Grace'

Lucid dreaming is the ability to be consciously awake within a dream state and to know that you are in a dream state as opposed to the awake reality of your day to day life.

Beautiful but telling, it's funny how dreams transpire. The fluidity of a dream state reality is a compounding force of knowledge.

In my dreams, the festival and festivities continued. Remember from the last dream state, the environment of the festival sort of moved in and around what felt like my own home and house. It was quite a humongous house with different wings, as it materialized in front of me and I went in to see my loved ones, family and friends all around, coupled with some artists/musicians from the festival.

I came across a childhood high school friend of mine whom I had just reunited with from outside the dream state in the awake reality. We were quite close in school and it moved me to happy tears when I found out he was also a successful musician, a celebrity in his own right.

I had memories of how I would escape the boarding house to meet him at parties in the wildest parts of Lagos city, Lagos Island, Obalende, Nigeria, West Africa. A city that never sleeps.

Our love for music was one of a kind and it was so compelling to see how we both turned out doing the things we loved the most.

Back in the dream, while speaking to my dear friend, a scenario that had been taken from the storage of my memory quickly played itself out and I was able to go straight to my pre-planned answers and reactions, exactly as if I was in the awake reality, This was something I pondered about while awake, going through a "what if scenario" and having a conclusion of responses, which now came true for me to experience in the dream.

As our discussion was about to finish, I noticed some strange and otherworldly beings in the same room with my loved ones and family.

I zoomed in and was able to see them clearly, they looked a bit like characters from the kid show called 'Teletubbies' but looked more humanoid. One of them had purple skin and the other had blue skin, similar to the native characters in the movie called 'The Avatar'.

This changed my state of mind and the festive atmosphere into a more scary and hostile one.

In an instant I realized that I was in a dream state reality, I became fully lucid but was still very afraid. Then I recognised the energies of these beings from previous dreams. They had very high energies that I often interpreted as hostile or out to get me somehow, I always would run and get chased by these beings in their different forms, either as a dog, the police, or a masquerade etc.

While still in the lucid dream, I remembered what I had learnt recently, that there was no light without darkness and no darkness without light. A yin-yang effect with two sides of a coin. (A perspective of the yin-yang effect states that in the darkness there's always a doorway to the light and in the light, there's always a doorway back to the darkness). They are interconnected and one cannot exist without the other.

I have come to understand this as two sides of a coin, the light and dark side and whichever side I choose (because we always have a choice) to base and operate my perspective from, would determine how I see and experience the manifestations in front of me that I have attracted or created. As this world is indeed an attraction based world, even an intrusion has to be somehow attracted and invited, chosen before experiencing, it is all-inclusive. The nature of the free will choice our universe works on, even though this free will choice depends ultimately on our belief systems, the programming and the ways we have been taught to see things and to be.

I was determined to practice and play with this phenomenon in my dream state reality until I totally exhausted my perspectives from the dark side of the coin, like fear, anger, worry, and more negative emotions, making it neutral and easy enough for me to choose how I want to truly experience any situation.

Back to the dream, at this point I was finally able to recognise the light side of the coin, a perspective attained through unconditional love and high spirits. I also noticed that this was the first time I could see and retain the colour of their skin, and since I was lucid and awake/aware within the dream, I fully remembered that my plan was to chase after these beings to collect more information as opposed to me running away.

For the first time, I could significantly recognise these beings for their unconditionally loving nature that they were. It was as if I was overfilled and overwhelmed with so much deep love coming from them and I was willing to explode in light. It was indeed a new sense to experience others having so much love for me, after all my mother was the only reference point I had for this type of unconditional love. I went after them and enjoyed the moments of hugs and deep love connections until somehow they disappeared and in another instance, as dreams endeavour to transpire, everything changed again.

But this time, it all changed to a more hostile atmosphere of some type of war and apocalyptic scenery, and I had also started losing my lucidity but was still fairly lucid as I decided to make my move, floating away as if to fly from the upstairs window of my building. Now I was outside and saw other beings making their way hurriedly fleeing from the turmoil, creatures of all shapes and sizes. And I seemed to also feel loved ones and others following my footsteps as I maneuvered my way in and around the atmosphere, heading towards the top of a hill along a fence line, as if I was being drawn to it.

I realized (manifested) some very large dinosaur-looking creatures in a herd on some green field at the right side of the fence line as I was floating towards the fence from the left side. At first glance, I thought they were out to get me as they were running very fast but seemed to run past me with ease. While in the middle of these graceful giants, I realized they only cared about getting to the same hill I was attracted to. I maneuvered and got ahead of them.

As I got to the bottom of the hill and started floating upwards, I realized something defining and striking. From the perspective of a high vantage point on the hill, I was bestowed with the sight of the totality of an apocalyptic reality that I no longer wished to be part of and was no longer interested in watching.

I felt untouchable as I floated up to the top of the mountain, where I found a completely different reality of peace, harmony, joy, tranquility and love.

This was indeed the home of these graceful giants and other light beings, who were heading back home from the turmoil to the top of the mountain of grace.

FOUR

PEACE

Dream Memories 17th May 2015
'Peaceful Resolutions'

What felt like a dream I now know I had dreamt once and many times before moving to The Republic of Ireland years ago, when I was still in somewhat of a dark place in my life, playing with darkness and fear. This is a dream I now truly understand because I was replaying the events of the dream, watching and learning from my reactions while in the dream. There was a part of me observing and co-ordinating while another part of me acted the role in the dream as if it were very real so as to get the most genuine reaction of emotions from energies within me that could be changed or released. This was a multifaceted dream with more than one level, with an awake observer that directs the dreamer to play out the dream.

I had the possibility to re-run the programme, if I felt I could do better in some aspects and bring more of it to the light. Each time I played it, there was more understanding and better choices made to transform the energies. This dream is a core and very good example of how we humans awaken and ascend as we evolve and we have the opportunity to do most of this work in our sleep state. I also remember using one of my superpower skills of flying with invisible wings to flee away from what I considered to be danger, *the other skill I remember using is my invisibility ability, whereby no one could see me but I was right there.*

The first play of the dream was what could be deemed a "nightmare", and there was much fear within my 3D (Third density, psychological, rational) mind. I woke up within the dream having finished analyzing the capacity of fear. I intended to replay the dream to change this energy of fear and to rewrite the programmes. I.e. find ways to reduce the fear in me or not to opt into fear in the first place.

I was realizing that fear is an illusion and the only thing truly feared is fear itself. The fear comes from the thought of the unknown happening and the danger that may or may not occur. Fear is fed either by the memory of past danger or failings, or the thought of future danger or failure. All coming from the illusion of time as in the past and the future, not happening at that particular moment, neither can be proven to exist at that moment, as they are only in the memory or thoughts.

Sometimes, even in the presence of what we would call danger, the fear is somehow not there or not paid attention to, as the mind goes into shock or practicality. (Hence the saying "You never really know what you will do until you are right in the so-called dangerous situation").

The storyline of the dream involved me being with a bunch of people on an adventure, partying from place to place. I remember being in buses and witnessing various street fights, people using different sharp objects and weapons. The platform or background/geography was set in The Republic of Ireland and partly Nigeria, the usual platforms I use within my dream matrixes and stemming from memories within my consciousness, due to my being in those areas of the world for most of my life.

A major character started to form and be clear to me. He was the worst of them all and turned out to be this elite millionaire club owner. I can remember him screaming out from his ego self saying, 'Don't you know I own the club?' Don't they know I own the club?".

I noticed that each time I re-played the dream programme or should I say "Game", I always tried to run away from him or hide, and he kept chasing me, the moment he noticed I acknowledged him and knew all his secrets.

This character was the epitome of a so-called "bad man", with so many atrocities committed in secret. He was a very defensive man who would do all in his power to hide the truth and to exercise power and authority on others, due to the magnitude of his own fear.

I sensed him having a second in command who always helped him to chase me. I can remember firstly having dangerous fights with some of his minions, then waking up briefly still within the general dream but at the top level, in order to prepare me and deploy me back again into the lower levels of the dream.

These re-runs of the dream storyline continued until I was able to interact with his minions using less fear and defense, and was even able to eventually change their minds and turn them into friendly beings that only wanted to party with me. But they were all still connected and working for the boss, which was probably how I was able to get all the dirty truths about his undercover operations.

I remember being on a bus with these minions and all hell would break loose, whereby there were weapons and rowdiness in the air. The first few trials of the dream involved either fear, fight or flight, like the survival instinct within our adrenal cortex. I would wake up from the same dream sweating and saying to myself that I needed to get back to the dream, as the desired outcome had not been met. Then I plunged back into the dream, and while in the dream I made sure not to be lucid so I could get the full effect of the dream leaning towards the transformational resolution, without any negative actions on my part.

My character in the dream had to be stripped of all the knowledge of knowing it was a dream. So on waking up, just before I was fully awake and before seeing myself on the bed, a different level of my consciousness will analyze the dream to assess how the character did, just like a middleman that had some sort of supervisory position. This same level of consciousness was also responsible for plunging and deploying my lower level character back into the dream, "like a boxing coach, telling its fighter to get back in the ring", for more trials so as to achieve the desired results.

And yet meanwhile, a much higher part of my consciousness just stayed vigilant as an observatory point that collected all information and enough details to allow me to play out the experiences and what I had learnt while in the awake reality, for the benefit of my soul.

Indeed, it came to a point where I realized I was able to transmutate, change, and neutralise fear too quickly. I wanted to continue this process as I was getting good at it, so I decided to add an element to the dream that allowed me to explore more of the fear energies in me, and to get the best out of releasing this, because I could sense that there were still, within my system, non-beneficial and heavy energies hidden in places I could not gain access to.

The element added to the dream sequence was my little baby boy, and then the dream got more serious. My wife and my son were sleeping on the same bed as myself, we were in a hotel in Houston, Texas, USA, and anytime I woke up back on the bed into the awake reality, I always had the comfort of my wife and my just 10 month old son, sleeping beside me before I would plunge back into the same dream.

When I unleashed myself in the dream, this time with the twist of carrying my ten month old baby boy into this chaotic environment, I 'the character' seemed to have gone rogue, suspecting anything I came across and even manifesting weapons to attack from a defensive point of view.

My son was sleeping next to me, in the awake reality, so it was easy to fit him into the dream, but the effect was so strong that I commenced obliterating anything that moved in a way I did not like, and from a fearful point of view this was everything. Which defeated the purpose of my original intention because I became the monster instead.

So, I downplayed the character (representing myself) and turned him into an embryo. He kind of looked like a tadpole that, in later re-runs of the dream, became a little toad or frog that was sacred and that I had to protect (The Frog Prince).

I kept throwing him in crevices or safe places when I felt danger or would run away with him (I can picture a funny cartoon image of me running like the 'Benny Hill Show', looking backwards always with a toad in my hand).

I remember trying to escape through the window when I got spotted in the club.

I remember being in the presence of the elite club owner and his partner, the second in command. I could not stand his energy, but I was able to feel how scared and confused he was and ready to enact violence from his own defensive standpoint. It was indeed very difficult to get this character to see the light and change. I kept running away for my dear life anytime I realized there was no talking to this guy, he was blinded and bent on protecting himself by getting rid of all threats he came across. *This kind of reminded me of myself when I had the full energy of my son's character.*

I realized this was a pivotal place for me so I kept on working on this part of the programme over and over again as my intention and goal was not to kill or fight anyone as a result of being protective and also not to flee away. I was to stay there till the end without fear, having resolved all issues.

I got to the point where I was able to sway most of his minions and even the second in command towards the light, as I was able to now see them as playful characters and not threatening ones. We were all now exploring parties and journeys together but as regards the energy of the boss, I could either be hidden or they were pretending to chase me because it was becoming more clear that the boss was not able to change at this time and would go after them, particularly if he knew about them turning to the light.

On my final journey after getting back my toad, I hid in a safe place while also sneaking away from the boss, until he saw me fleeing through the window again with my toad on my palm.

I felt much distress, hate, and struggles, heavy emotions emanating from him. As his empire was crumbling from within, he could feel that he had lost the war and was losing every other remaining battle but he was still determined to fight to the last.

I developed a sense of pity and respect for him, as I knew he could not be influenced to change, as that was not part of his path and journey. I found myself on a traveling van filled with friendly beings cruising the beautiful nature of a place with red sand that looked and felt like we were within a remote village in Africa.

As my eyes gazed on this beautiful building with what looked like a transparent and very spacious front room, the tour guide advised that this was the house of their king. I was amazed and felt very honoured to see this and be there.

I do not remember having my toad with me, but I just remembered that it was such a happy ending and feeling. And I was waking up fully with very clear intentions to bring all this information and understanding back to the 3d "3rd density" matrix of the human earth collective, which is the so-called 'awake reality'.

I was also blessed with other downloads and information from other levels of my consciousness just after waking up, as I was still present as a multidimensional being.

1. *I got a message from a famous radio DJ in Ireland on how he is much more in support of myself and my sister as a band since he was not able to do much while he was alive. He died five years ago but we did not know this until recently.*

   I told my friend that DJ Tony D emailed us a few months ago and recommended us to various outlets through a social and business network called "LinkedIn" and others. My jaw dropped when he said, "He died 5 years ago". It was a similar image to him that I have used to represent the boss of an elite club owner millionaire.

2. *I was in a channeling session with Archangel Michael, who shed some light on the elites of the world still trying to hold on to their control and manipulation of the world using channels in Africa, creating more havoc even though they had lost the war and all their battles seemed to be failing at the end. We all laughed about it as he said, "But they are trying really hard, we can give them that".*

   I grew up in Africa, so I sent my love, light and healing straight to those situations and advised the elites to take a break, have a KitKat and give it a rest. As we had all created this illusionary game and it is well overdue for the next stage, moving away from the extreme polarities into a more loving neutrality, for we are all one.

I will now elaborate on what a channeling session is. This is simply the bringing forth of supposedly broader perspective information through a being who is acting as the channel or some sort of medium.

We actually all do this on a day to day basis, i.e. bringing forth information from our brains or should I say, different levels of the mind such as the "subconscious and unconscious". The perspective from this information broadens once this information comes through from the heart or other multidimensional vibrational fields, as there is much wisdom here and the information is expansive and potentially non-judgemental, not being tainted by the polarities of the mind, so the mind becomes just a clear conduit translating the block of feelings into words, sounds or actions. A virgin mind that then births the Christ consciousness.

The heart is a powerhouse and functions as a connecting point of all things in existence within consciousness, from a human perspective, and it is also a path or way to the sub and unconscious mind and beyond, where we can receive information from the universe, stored in akashic records etc.

With a broad and expansive imagination and belief system, I and those with similar beliefs and knowledge, through phenomenal and life-changing experiences, can enjoy the luxury of communing and communicating with the likes of angels, spirits from life after death, extraterrestrial beings, nature and more.

Yes, I even go as far as communicating with trees, stones, crystals and other so-called inanimate objects, as they, too are part of the grand scheme of consciousness. There is deep wisdom and unconditional love within them.

FIVE

CONFLICT AND ANGER

Dream Memories 25th May 2015

Before this particular dream, I had a day where I was confronted by one of my 3D (third-dimensional) psychological programmes I had been trying to let go of, transmute or evolve.

I received a call from a character who served as a mirror of energy within me that I still had a little conflict with after much work. This character served as a belief system with restrictive or negative connotations according to my perceptions and this did not resonate with me. What made this more difficult for me was that my family and I had initially accepted this character to live under the same roof as me. This had been ongoing for a very long time so there was a constant reminder of what I did not resonate with.

Each time I encountered a clash with this energy, it served as a tool for growth. I would always go through a healing process that led to the expansion of my soul and more understanding of things and my so-called self.

I was fully aware that the outcome was for me to understand, accept and love this unique divine being regardless, as part of my unconditional love practices. This was a character I have come to appreciate and thank for choosing to play this role for the sake of my own expansion and evolution. It was not an easy task but

I had come to a place of understanding, a place I could call the final stages of transmutation, where I could neutralize this energy within me much more easily.

As the call from this energy came, I realized there was still a little bit of resentment that was felt strongly, only for a short while, before moving to a much clearer understanding and light energy of love. This character had displayed a lot of judgment, criticism and dislike for my own uniqueness.

And my own psychological ego personality sometimes fought back, totally blinded within the moment to the fact that the character was only reflecting and serving as a mirror for me. This was all happening within me as an energy of conflict that I had to resolve and transmute.

In a way, I was the one judging myself, and sometimes my psychological ego personality/physical self would push for the option of ignoring these characters and accepting myself. But this was easier said than done and was never enough. Sometimes I wished that the characters would leave as maybe if they were far away, it would be much easier to accept and love them from afar, which was a possibility. But the more they remained close, the more I knew this was really something I had to work out within myself and fully understand because even if they left, I would still not be able to run away from myself. Without this energy within me being fully resolved, there would be yet another dear soul coming to act as a character, attracted by the energy within me, giving me once again the opportunity to fully resolve the energy and to reveal the blessings and understanding hidden within this life experience.

After the phone call, I decided it was time to work on this energy in my dream state and to find final resolutions.

Later that night, I found myself in a dream state again. The location was my family house, where I was with various family members, even those who did not truly live there were also present.

It felt like a very loving and peaceful environment until I ventured into a room which I could call my personal space within the family house, and there they were, two of them, characters I did not resonate with, laying under the blankets of my bed. It was as if the main character had invited a friend to come and live in the house without the house owner's permission. As though they figured that I was getting the hang of things so they needed to double up to have a better chance of irritating me or pissing me off. Nonetheless, I found again the conflict energy, within me, that I needed to work on.

At first, they were very relaxed and were using all of my personal artifacts. None of this bothered me, as I nicely greeted them and the newcomer by saying "hello" and "welcome". I proceeded and left my room to find another room that might be vacant in the house so I could do what needed to get done, but there was no more space left in the house, every other room was already occupied.

Everything was going so well, and I was almost like a saint until I realized that I had been kicked out of my own house. The 'catch twenty-two' was that I really needed to finish what I was doing then, but instead. I worked on myself and found peace as I decided to manage the situation. I thought to myself, 'this is a temporary situation and it is good to be nice, as these people do not have anywhere else to go, so they are welcome to stay'.

I would go back to the room, stay on the floor and finish whatever business I had to finish. I found myself on the floor of my room, sitting down with my back to the end of the bed, headphones on, as I continued to work on my computer as planned, and then it finally happened.

I received a tap on the back of my head from one of the character's feet as they were lying on the bed above me at my back. It was the newcomer, she said 'you are disturbing us, we are trying to discuss private issues and do not want you to hear what we are saying'.

At first, I felt very perplexed and did not know how to respond to this, and then I started feeling the so-called conflict energy now rising from within me. The ladies continued to talk and then went into criticizing me, my beliefs and my way of living. It was getting really heated but I was determined to keep my cool and not let it all get to me, and then I realized the truth of the matter was that I was already there and within the eye of this storm, doing my best not to explode physically and psychologically.

I aimed to be peaceful, practiced my deep breathing and kept my calm. I advised them that they should not worry because I had my earphones on and would not hear any private matters they had to discuss. I was deep into what I was doing and they would not even know I was there. To my surprise, they refused and wanted me out of my own room. They kept rambling, judging and criticizing until I lost control of myself and got fully immersed in anger and strongly within the so-called conflict energy that had now risen fully to the surface. I became like a monster shouting at the top of my voice for both of them to leave the house immediately and explaining how ungrateful they had been after all the help we had given to them. They both refused to even get off the bed and then the newcomer started to threaten violence.

This was meant to provoke the fear that was in me, but because I had been working on exposing all my fears and letting them go, deeming them as irrelevant, I do not easily go into a fear based reality of action/reaction. The entire dream stopped in a pause as if it was time for me to take a breather, my subconscious mind had proposed a programme of fear for me to enter but I did not choose to go there. This allowed me to realize with a certain lucidity, that this was all a dream and an opportunity for me to work on and fully know the conflicted energies within me. I had intended this experience and I knew that everything projected outward and externally could be called illusions, while our inner selves possessed the true reality. At this point, I was back in the dream, and the newcomer had already stabbed one of the family members. I smiled and they were healed immediately. I called the authorities to remove the newcomer from the house, not to punish or prosecute them, but to place them in a rehabilitated safe house. At this point, the newcomer was threatening to burn down the house.

Through this whole experience, I was able to show forgiveness and much love to the main character. Also at this point, she showed much remorse, love and gratitude back to the family.

It was a resolution I was able to feel deep within me. I had a very high understanding of the irrelevance of judgment and criticism, whether it was being directed at me or through me. At this point, it was very laughable and a very great feeling to be on top of these feelings and overall that, for I now knew it was all just illusions, and the conflict within me was fully seen for the illusion that it was.

The dream then continued on to a different scenario. This time I was literally floating with joy and ecstasy, visiting places and meeting loved ones outside, little details of memory until a unique point where I was floating on a bridge over a city lake or canal filled with much vegetation and pollution. There were many beings around and I can remember most of us were forming groups and helping to clean up certain streets around. I remember getting on a spaceship that seemed to be helping with the cleaning of the pollution from above. I also remember getting off this ship and floating down to help a group of people who were chasing some cows, as if to save them. The cows looked pretty mad.

I then realized this was not the first time I would have a similar dream of people trying to save cows running beside the lake. I helped to save a cow and floated towards the bridge in front of me while looking at some alien beings floating in and out of their spaceships with devices cleaning up the weather and environment.

These beings looked like the alien race they call the "Greys", but they were taller. Alternatively, they might have been the "Clears", a similar but different alien race. There was also a "Yahyel" presence.

The Yahyels are a hybrid race between Humans and the extraterrestrials called the Greys. The Greys are believed to be a possible future and timeline of a path taken by humanity, while embarking on a technological and super mind based evolution. They are believed to have come from the future and back to the past, where we are now, to collect DNA materials in order to create a new race of hybrids for the continuation of their existence, because they had already done away with most of their original physical human DNA contents. This was because they were more aligned with technology and metaphysics, and were advanced in their evolution. So these beings are experienced and seen to be super intelligent.

Even the phenomenon of alien abductions was believed to be perpetuated mostly by these beings, so that they could study and explore humanity, as well as retrieve human DNA as part of an agreement between souls. Unfortunately, these beings had lost most of their emotional aspects, so they were not at all sensitive towards the fears of the humans they abducted or came in contact with.

Since humans are in the game of forgetfulness and would not remember or adhere to a soul contract already agreed upon, these beings felt it necessary to abduct.

And as fear is the pivotal energy that stops us from investigating the darkness that exists, we can remember and shed light on other parts of our consciousness, only like the extraterrestrials.

Consciousness in all its entirety is one big source that can never be separated from itself except only by powerful illusions, which we perceive and experience as real.

This is why it seems as if we are all so many different kinds of consciousness, where in actual fact and in its core essence, there is only one, and we are all using that same one consciousness, in the many different ways possible.

In considering consciousness as one, this means that the aliens and extraterrestrials are just other facets of the same unified consciousness that we are. This also means that every other human or living thing you see is just another version of you because it is the same consciousness that is appearing and playing out within that particular conduit of expression.

I understand some people may prefer to remain in a belief system where the consciousness stays separate. This way, they can continue to experience dis-unity whereby only their Individuality is felt primarily. The individual is the greatest illusion of all and from this, all other illusions and even delusions are created. These include insecurity, Isolation and frustration.

Humanity has been stuck within the illusionary box of a survival mode, characterised by, "We fear what we do not understand or can not see". A mode carried from 'for example' the time of the dinosaurs, whereby the fear of being eaten was a real prospect, and experience carried through our evolutionary process as humans.

After all of this dream sequence, I floated back to the place where I woke up on my bed.

The next night after the dream around 2am, I woke up and went out to my cousin's balcony in Houston, Texas. I started looking at and into the sky. I had not seen it that clear and beautiful since I visited the USA. There were stars in all the spaces of the sky like trillions of stars, I stayed and gazed for a while as this was very beautiful, and there it was, another triangular spaceship with orange lights at the three points in front of me, as it floated gracefully sideways. It stopped for a while as I waved and was filled with joy that I was able to witness such a phenomenon.

SIX

INCARNATIONS

Dream Memories 27th May 2015

In this dream, it felt like I was my oversoul again. *Over-Soul means the house, database or collective of souls you have been, will be or are engaged with from the perspective of your singular individual nodal point of existence.* Your I AM in your current incarnation.

Except, this time, with the experience of collecting all my life incarnations after physical death and choosing a new vessel to reincarnate into. A great play of consciousness.

This felt like the most joyous feeling I had ever felt, the feeling of unconditional love coupled with my highest excitement, similar to but way stronger than the feeling of falling in love. It felt so good and very interesting to get all the new experiences from one life and incorporate them into the whole, followed by the adventure of choosing a new incarnation for more explorations and expansion. This greatly depends on the blueprint of the life to be had, and choices from what world, family, country and themes, even the necessity of being born with a disposition or skill sets that allow for certain tasks to be achieved imminently.

The whole experience felt so great and multidimensional that it is very difficult to explain in a one-dimensional or linear fashion with my 3D "Third density- Fourth-dimensional earthly mind".

At one point, it was as if I had placed multiple buckets under nectar trees and was simultaneously collecting the filled up buckets of different varieties of sweet nectar at the same time. What greatness in the abundance and concentration of joy and life, with sweet words, cannot explain.

I could sense I had a very substantial vacuum of consciousness that vastly extended for each bucket of nectar I collected, and it was also from this vast unique consciousness that I would fashion a new type of bucket to collect some new and specific types of nectar from unique kinds of nectar trees. *The buckets being the physical body or etheric light bodies in the case of life or existence created without any sort of physicality involved. And the variety of nectar being the different life experiences gained from the nectar trees, which are the different formations of worlds or realms I chose to explore.*

The dream then zoomed into one of my incarnations with light memories of the details until I found myself in front of a man who looked biologically more from the Asian "Indian" part of the world. There was a pillar on the left side while he was sitting on a high stool by the right. He was looking at and discussing with a very high vibrational being standing humbly by the pillar. This being was feminine like, with pale skin and it was as if this beautiful white light glowed like millions of stars through her. She was so attractive and I was drawn to join their conversation. She spoke so gently, beautifully and with so much love and regard. I knew I was indeed in the presence of an angel.

The gentleman was discussing his current incarnation and the difficult experiences he and his peers had to undergo, and how they were able to achieve success. The angel repeated very gently and lovingly with a beautiful smile that, yes, he was in the core forefront of the collective "world" experience, hence the steep trials he had chosen to experience and overcome. I, in turn, said "here here" as if to be in total understanding and to go with the flow of what was being said.

The man turned to me with almost a serious face and I replied that I was very glad to have chosen not as much of a steep experience as he had. He replied by saying, now that he has overcome this, he is also very happy that he has chosen this path due to the vastness of knowledge and wisdom he has attained.

The angel then went on to give us a magical profound transformational message.

Magical Profound Message:

For those within the core forefront and in the steep end, at any moment, to picture and feel this experience as the most important and exciting moment that they would ever go through in their life and to allow this moment to flow while being 100% within it and in the love of it. This can magically transform any moment into a highly vibrational, happy and loving one.

This stayed with me as I woke up and was filled with bliss with a beautiful smile on my face, as I could also still feel her presence in my room.

I then got a text message and wanted to ignore it because, in the past, a message from this certain individual brought me a lower vibrational energy and feeling, but the angel encouraged me to look at the message. It came from one of my earthly sisters who recently sent a fear based message to the family chat group, but no one in the family paid any attention to it. I had so much concern for her and wanted to help her physically but had learned from the past that this would only provoke and allow her to defend more of her fear based truths, which were indeed true within the reality she was choosing to live in. So not giving air-time or support to these types of messages was the best thing all in the family could do. My hesitation to open up the message was also accompanied by light and wisdom from the angel who was encouraging me to look at it. Even if it happens to be a continuation of a fear based idea, I will be able to address this and give knowledge and wisdom to my sister, from a standpoint of acceptance and unconditional love.

The words that came from the angel were so very powerful and profound that I was amazed and quickly moved into a different room and opened up the message, which was a video message. I did not want to wake up others who were sleeping.

To my surprise, it was a comedy about Adam and Eve in the bible, with very funny attributes about women and men. I laughed so hard, and the angel advised me to support my sister by letting her know how funny the video was and how she had made the whole family so happy by waking us up with laughter, indicating that this type of joyous reality is what we want and support.

This was an assurance for me that I did not need to save my sister or anyone else for that matter, as they are all part of God's source or overall consciousness and can find their way to the light by themselves because the light is truly what they are, but they have all forgotten this. All I needed to do was to show them respect for the choices they were making and love them unconditionally.

The beautiful name of "Sananda" followed the angel. This name is connected to the soul of "Yeshua ben Joseph", the one we know as Jesus Christ and the "Asin family of light" within the house of David.

I also felt the energy of Archangel Gabrielle, or rather, "The feminine perspective of the Archangel Gabriel".

SEVEN

THE SELFISH HUMAN LOVE

Dream Memories 9th June 2015

I found myself moving through some awkward buildings within hills and rocks. It appeared I was not the only one, there were so many people running helter skelter, trying to take cover as gunshots and even rockets were being fired towards that vicinity. It started very peacefully as we had all just finished up from an event and were joyously moving towards what seemed to be beautiful fields and peaceful land, but once the shooting started, this environment had to be changed by my "dreams matrix".

I realized that the shooting was done by only one person, who happened to be a childhood friend of mine whom I went to high school with. He was up a hill at a vantage point and I was able to zoom in and out of his position without physically moving closer. He was really angry and determined that everything he did was justifiable.

I tried to negotiate with him but he let me know that he had had enough of the people of the world.

He was convinced that most were just here to serve a purpose of their own selfish ego and did not really care or acknowledge the standpoint of others.

He considered himself as too many times a victim in the world and decided he would destroy whosoever he could, acting out on this overwhelming emotion and conclusion. He looked at me and had a bit of resonance about our friendship, then warned me to get out of the way and save who else I could because, for him, it was already too late.

After the telepathic discussion with him, I found myself very sympathetic but I moved swiftly to save whom I could and get away from all his crossfires.

In the next part of the dream, I found myself going to another event, sort of like a birthday of another friend, whereby you had to climb a funny staircase and then go down a different one to get to the actual room where the party was happening. I came across familiar faces greeting, and making my acquaintance until I got to the birthday boy and his friends. After all the well wishes and pleasantries, they continued with their condolences on the death of my friend, shooting from the vantage point of the mountain. He had been neglected of love and this had given him the opportunity to commit such atrocities and also to die in the process.

My dream friends realized that even if you are creating your own reality within your own universe, everything you see within this matters, for you to acknowledge and accept everything. Because it sums up the totality of you within that universe, and also, to show love to every part of it would be to show love to the totality of yourself at that point in time, within that universe.

So unity is very prevalent in the existence of the whole. My dear friend sacrificed his life and took other people's lives just to teach this. We all agreed on this fact and I advised them that I was not even aware that he had lost his life in the process. We went on to enjoy the rest of the party before I woke up.

The Love of Self 'For Self' Versus the Love of Self 'For All'

To love thyself for the benefit of only thyself in comparison to the love of thyself for the benefit of the whole totality of existence. The latter allows for the overall wholesome completion and continuation of the cycle, so it never runs stale, as opposed to love for only thyself, which can become restrictive towards divine light, stagnant and may most likely brew 'Dis-ease' as interruptions of ease and flow.

This dis-ease manifests in feelings of separation. Or when one does not extend love to other parts or representations of oneself, due to the ignorance of not knowing that all are from the same one 'Source' and that separation is only an illusion.

A practitioner of 'love of self for all' makes sure that love is first concentrated on the inside, cultivating a healthy practice towards love for the self, whereby they are now in the best position to give a hundred percent towards loving others, this way everybody wins, and the cycle is completed once the love that is put out, comes back with gained momentum towards the sender, exercising the universal law of Karma, 'What you put out, you get back'. You always reap what you sow.

EIGHT

SUSPICIOUS MIND

Dream Memories 1st July 2015

I found myself in my house with a lot of people talking and yapping away,, and it appeared as if we had just had a party. I went into my room and overheard a discussion between a few younger looking groups of people, and what caught my ears was the mention of metaphysical words like 3d, 4d, downloads and enlightenment. I figured these were kindred spirits and I gravitated towards all of them as I found them interesting. Different conversations started and I found myself moving all around the house with new friends talking and yapping away, and having a great time.

Then something happened. I seemed to have spilt a great deal of my drink on one of them, as I can remember. It went all over his shirt and he just stayed still and sturdy looking at me. I had just mistakenly painted his light striped long-sleeved shirt with red wine. I quickly owned up to it and advised him to come with me to choose a replacement from my newly bought long-sleeved shirts. I proceeded to sort them out from the wardrobe, bringing them out one by one for him to choose which one he preferred. I even intended to give him more than one if he wished.

I then stumbled on one of the shirts with something stashed in its breast pocket, and it turned out to be money, fifty pound notes, to be precise. At this point, I could feel myself creating something to hide the fact that I had money lying around. A type of stone manifested in the pocket and I could feel myself resizing it to make it large enough to hide the money in it due to a lack of trust and fear of robbery.

I quickly realized that I should not have this fear but I went on with the play of things. I heard a question from one of the characters in the room asking, "What is in there?, There's something in there". I replied to them that it was just one of my loyal stones, as I touched the stone embracing it within the pocket. I left the shirt in the wardrobe, took about five other shirts and placed them on a platform for him to choose from.

The night continued and it dawned on me that I now had a suspicious self, my reality was now split and I was also suspicious of the characters, even though they were kindred spirits. I tried not to let this get in the way of my enjoyment as we continued to have fun throughout the night.

Morning came and I found myself floating outside to meet up with the guests who apparently traveled from faraway places, from countries like the UK, USA, and Australia and were all now making their way to the airport to fly back home.

I was happily floating as I arrived at the car, to wish them my final farewell. As I had my head in the car window chatting and bidding farewell, I realized a conflicted energy within me, so I moved out and saw that the car was mine and they intended to drive this to the airport without my consent.

Even though I noticed this creation started from my suspicious energy, the feeling of betrayal was stronger and I acted out to defend myself and make sure I was not left without a car. I reasoned and discussed it with them and could see their disappointment about the situation but they were still banked on struggling with me about the car keys. I then reached for my phone and called the police who came immediately, instead of getting them in trouble, I advised the police to help get my guests to the airport as they were from far away and had been having a very good time, they were unable to drive or think straight due to the amount of alcohol in their system. I made a joke to the police saying that one of my guests, who does not even know how to drive (and where he lives, they drive on the other side of the road), has promised the rest of the guests that he will take them to the airport, so he got my car keys and decided to do this anyway. The policeman smiled and at this moment I woke up.

This dream showed me the following:

1. *I was able to manifest a stone in my pocket to cover up the money there and also able to manipulate and change the size of the stone, showing me the ease with which we can create objects to appear from thin air without thinking twice about it, once we are put in situations we might deem as extreme. It strengthened my belief that this same power of materialization we have in dreams can also be done in the so-called "real life" awake reality.*

2. *Apart from the fact that anything that is not on the positive side stems from fear, I got the strong sense that once I activated an energy feeling of suspicion within me, it affected the outward external scenario whereby the characters somehow turned from a very high vibrational good type to the ones that will actually carry out the deeds to which I suspected them of, following suite from the inner feelings I had, which also strengthened my belief that you create your own reality*

from within as your resonant feelings and thoughts are what is then projected and then manifested outwardly for you to see and experience. It can even be as powerful as changing the characters of those you attract. This also supports the saying, "Be careful what you wish for or you might just get it". I decided to strengthen my trust and faith in the source God that 'all is well', 'all the time'.

NINE

FEAR

Dream Memories 2nd August 2015

Right before I went to sleep on this particular evening, I listened to a Channeling session. It was the teachings of Jesus Christ, about how fear and doubts are our worst enemies. *We are able to make fear our best friend by exploring it, until we realize how irrelevant it is in most cases and can then release it from our vibration system, to let it go, as opposed to avoiding or running away from it, thereby keeping it within our system. The fear consists of the restrictions and boxes we keep ourselves in the physical reality. This fear is what we use to shoot ourselves in the foot when it comes to what we desire and want.*

Jesus refreshed the vibration and energy of our connection to "All that is or the ONE source", as we are all interconnected nodes forming one pure source of energy, which some call "God". He advised us about the perfection we have through this pure light and love, and also how staying in a positive and unrestricted state at all times keeps us fully connected to the light.

He performed some healing miracles and connected directly to the ONE source to deliver a message and understanding to someone in the room who was stuck on their path. It was a wonderful feeling to be present and to watch a true master in action as he described how he was connecting with energy all the way from the beginning of time. It was as if everyone present just got swept up in that energy, it was very intoxicating, beautiful and the most wonderful feeling of peace, resolution, tranquility and belonging. It was as if the energy was pulling every fiber of my being and nothing else had ever felt so right and good.

Here I am now, on my bed and still enjoying this wonderfully tranquil and joyous feeling, and in a flash, the mind quickly moved towards lower vibrational thoughts that were fear based, but I quickly incorporated and integrated higher vibrational feelings, like laughter, as I could realize the fears were just lies I had bought into and created as programmes in my subconscious. I was very glad to release these no longer serving energies.

A dream began as I slept. My son and a couple of other family members were in a building that was partly my home and partly had some sort of public access to public functions.

It then shifted to a fear based dream where the people were running away or hiding from something and I myself was in it as a protector, due to my understanding that the dream was all an illusion, and it just felt so real. So in the beginning, I had just enough lucidity to effect this.

My building now appeared to be a safe house and a sacred place, as there was destruction and war going on outside. More and more people escaped into the building to take refuge, each bringing their fears. Whoever was chasing them wandered around the building looking for ways to get in and get them.

It was a scene of chaos out there with different types of alien beings flying on different modalities of craft. Many were even using chemical warfare and mind control devices on those who harbored fear and who doubted their own survival and sovereignty.

I can remember some of the perpetrators on some sort of flying motorcycle that had fire coming out of the back and front of it, spitting this out at will to target those running away from them. A lot of the time I could feel some fear creeping inside of me, as this was so much in the people around me, which allowed some of these alien beings to find the energy and attach themselves to and infiltrate the sacred building.

Each time the dynamics of the building would change and I would realize a suppressor was in front of me within the building. I would quickly drop all the fears and fill the whole building with a lot of love, changing the suppressor beings into more light and harmless beings. I would then invite them to stay in this new way or leave and never come back, if their choice was to stay in darkness.

I understood this process would continue due to the amount of fear harbored by those in the house. So I decided to go around discussing, uplifting and inspiring people to get rid of their fears, so that we can extend this safe house under the white light to more and more places within the planet and end the chaos and war out there. I realized how difficult this was for some people due to the type of belief systems they had carried for very long periods.

Some of them were just not able to control their fear and allowed the dark beings to infiltrate and take them away from the safe house. As some watched this, they determined to work on, understand and release their fears because even if they got taken away, fear would not help them and without fear they had the strongest chance of surviving the war.

They trusted in the safe house as their connection to their highest self, the source of all things, knowing that, from the highest or broadest perspective, nothing can go wrong as they are the creator of all things.

It was a very interesting dream, as I moved all around the building, floating and doing my best to save people from their fears and then also encountering the suppressors, each time seeing them flee with anger or fear and even sometimes with laughter, as the light in the safe house spread and grew stronger. Some ended up staying for a while and having a very meaningful conversation with me before choosing to go back to the darkness, while some totally transformed and stayed in the light as helpers.

My conversations with them went very deep, as they explained their understanding and role within the overall experience as being one of serving a higher purpose of polarity, to offer the darkness for the souls within the human collective who have all chosen to come and explore the positive and negative within the 3rd density, "3d Planet Earth".

Sometimes as the energy of fear grew and got me into a confused state, I would find myself waking up briefly as if to get some air and catch my breath, before going back deep into the waters. Back into the dream where at this time, I would become fully aware of my "I AM" God source within my multidimensional higher self, and the power and light within this eternal unconditional love.

Even when I finally woke up, the feeling of the dream was very strong as I played with my son and wife discussing and retrieving the memories from the dream. Apparently, unbeknown to me, she, too, was going through some sort of similar dream where she had to face her fears, understand them and let them go.

I connected fully to my "I AM" God source within my multidimensional higher self as I jumped into another dream where I met a lot of family and friends, showing them the light of the source, and advising that it did not matter what anyone else said, they too can tap into and find this light in them with no restrictions so they too can shine the brightest. It was a wonderful feeling this time, as I went back to the same safe house, which had now extended and turned into a vast community of light and love. Let's just say I got many hugs and kisses, for there was only love around everywhere.

TEN

POWER OF FEAR

Dream Memories 3rd August 2015

In describing this particular dream, I would say it was like an exercise drill for physical fitness and mental development in that it exposed me to some of my fears yet again, and helped me get over them, fears that were still deep inside of me. I had not been given the opportunity in my awake physical reality/life to deal with these fears.

The dream was set in a very beautiful rocky scenario with different jagged and rough hills to climb. There was beautiful greenery and flowers growing in between them, and also lakes and waters below, also different types of land marsh and even a beach. Even though this looked very much like natural scenery, it was kind of closed, sort of like the gladiator-style arenas. It also might have been an island of some sort, my inner feeling tells me it was either a spaceship or a place on hollow earth. It was a wonderful adventure climbing up and down the rocky terrain and the water down below did not seem to bother me. I thought to myself that I used to be very wary about this because I never swam before, so the fear of drowning always came to mind in the past.

But in this very moment, I was very glad to see that I had no fear and any time I found myself in the water, I remained okay and I explored and found my way out to continue climbing, until something new was introduced in the sequence.

In the waters appeared various types of creatures like snakes and crocodiles, as well as other very beautiful and wild animals, moving all around or resting in specific places on the dry areas of the mountain.

This further tested my state of fear. But firstly, I was mingling with the natives or teachers there who helped with directions and the likes, we even had beautiful conversations and enjoyment with some sort of otherworldly beings that looked like Lions, Bears and other earthly animals but they were also highly intelligent and looked like humanoid beings, until something changed.

I seemed to have struck a chord of great fear within me, and this shifted my entire reality into one of great fear and chaos, whereby I started to run away and evade the Lion and Bear beings.

Also, these beings seemed to have changed back into the usual wild animals we have on earth, thereby evoking my fear of wild animals.

I would sometimes meet their cubs and quickly jump to the conclusion and fear that their mother must be around somewhere and would be charging towards me. This experience then gets created whereby I see myself and others running for dear life and trying not to fall into the water due to the presence of the wild animals.

The fear now introduced made everything seem so primitive. These used to be wonderful, beautiful and highly intelligent beings that I could have learnt a lot from, but instead my fear had turned them into ferocious beasts that we had to protect ourselves from, as we have learnt from our own primitive survival skills.

Sometimes we would catch a break from the fear while being guided by the natives or teachers who brought us very close to these beings so we could interact with them. This sometimes worked and sometimes failed, however, as fear took over by chasing us all around the mountains again. In time it became like a game that was quite interesting and we would plan our routes very properly so as not to reach a dead end, where we would have to interact with the mountain beings or fall into the water to face the water beings.

This continued until we eventually found our way out to the nearby beach and then I was given a task to sweep a very large area by taking off the loiter and the dirt, making the beach cleaner for those having fun on it.

I remembered that I had had similar roles or tasks while I was in high school and I told them it was going to be easy as a piece of cake. I started sweeping the floor, sand and some other parts made of artificial concrete, I then started realizing how huge the task was because I did not feel right only cleaning up a few sections when looking at how clean they were while other places were dirty, so I decided to clean it all.

I saw so many beings joyously walking around enjoying their day on the beach and this made me feel really happy cleaning it for them.

And as I continued, I started to move faster because I realized my time was running out and my transport for leaving the lovely Island was already there so I kept sweeping last with my broom until I woke up.

I remember before I slept that night, having a chat with an archangel called "Archangel Raphael". I requested more of his wonderful healing energies, and to help me with my psychic abilities which seemed to be improving fast in some areas. I also called upon the ascended masters to take me to one of their healing retreats, ships or places, places I believe were the source of my dream locations. These higher dimensional beings are representatives of my own inner and higher multidimensional selves. I can remember having three different dreams that night, the second one I will discuss in the next chapter but the third one was really for my own inner and private amusement and core healing. Therefore, I did not wish to recall all memories but retained all the wonderful feelings and energies.

Fear

Fear is the most powerful sensation, feeling or emotion and can create realities whereby the energies are polarised in a negative direction. Fear sets the premise for all other negative emotions or feelings like sadness, hate, doubt and the like.

Fear is created when the divine light within unconditional love is covered and hidden with the illusion of darkness. This is why they say, "We fear what we cannot see or what we do not understand". Without the light, we cannot see, and also without intelligence 'which is also seen as light', we are unable to understand.

Fear can only exist because darkness exists, and darkness exists due to the polarisation of light. It is as if something has been placed in the middle to split the core vibration and create the extreme opposite on one side, while the original is on the other side, just as two sides of a coin.

Let me give you a great example of this. Consider you are outside on a very sunny day, with the sun representing the core light and vibration, but once anything physical or material is put in the middle of that light, a sort of darkness is created and is called a shadow.

Now, we all know that the shadow is less real than the sun and can only exist because of the light coming from the sun. Since fear can only exist where there is darkness, it is even more of a greater delusion as it has its roots in darkness, an inferior part of light.

Unconditional love is the basis of everything in existence. The sun never bothers the flower, it shines regardless and no matter what the flower does, it still shows its love.

When the delusion of darkness is created due to the obstruction of the light within unconditional love, it becomes fear; it is then an opposite polarity.

Now it drags in all other aspects of negativity, as they can only exist and be experienced in this realm. Furthermore, due to its extreme nature, fear allows courage to come out of unconditional love, as its polar opposite.

Other than that, everything remains positive within unconditional love. If consciousness is left alone, the back of the coin with a negative charge ceases to reveal itself, as it pitters out once the momentum slows down. It all returns to the front side of the coin to be positively charged, since this is the side that mimics the original mode of energy before polarization happens.

What we know as love is merely powerful fragrances of feelings coming from unconditional love, but we have been conditioned to follow the narrative of set experiences. For example, the love for a friend ceases as soon as the friend becomes an enemy or the famous lover's rift we see in romance novels, with the act of falling in love but as soon as the relationship ends, a huge vacuum is left. A vacuum that invites uncertainties, yielding to the fact that the love is only temporary and valid as it is based on the condition that both parties stay in the relationship.

This is where we get to the feeling of "hate", the other opposite of love that many may find familiar. As fear is the opposite of unconditional love within a polarised spectrum, hate is the opposite of conditional love.

Hate takes its cues from its father 'fear', the same way as conditional love takes its cue from its mother 'unconditional love'.

Hate is what is left when divine light is taken away from conditional love through the delusion of darkness. We call this phenomenon a delusion because true divine light is untouchable and can never be taken away, unless we have made it appear to be so through an illusion, polarising it into 'have' and 'have nots', so we can experience the 'have nots' and see how it would feel if there was no divine light.

Fear is also a kind of conditional deluded love, a unique one in its own right since everything comes from the base emotion and energy of the cosmos, that of "unconditional love". Unconditional love consists of total and complete freedom, allowance, respect, care, regards and adoration with no restrictions whatsoever, promoting union, progress, and construction, while fear is conditioned to restrictions only as it appears from a restriction of divine light, or at least the illusion of this and disappears once the attention focuses back on divine light. Fear tears things apart and promotes separation, retreat, and destruction.

The 'Shadow' darkness can only be as powerful as you make it to be because it is made out of you. I prefer that mine remains inactive, a shadow that never bothers anybody, at some point fear will comply by dissipating. If fear comes, it comes, but then look around you, is there any imminent danger? If the answer is 'No', then let the fear go! Look for something else to engage your attention. All is well.

The fear is just there to deliver a divine message, that you have strayed away from divine light and the true reality, so all you need to do is focus your attention back on divine light and love.

Let us explore this further and look at a non-polarised duality, that of gender with the "Feminine and Masculine energies".

The father's power is decision, while the mother's power is creation. The father decides what should be and the mother allows it to be. One of the highest dualities in all things, a masculine thought can be to protect the feminine because without the feminine, nothing can truly be experienced as existence, all will be just thoughts and there will be no depth of creation. The feminine needs the masculine for ideas to form, light is activated and turns into electricity in motion, ones and zeros on and off, forming its rhythm of waves from within the ocean of consciousness for the purpose of creation, consciousness and creation now being the ultimate form of life.

On the masculine side, the higher mental "God mind" of the universe decides through its thoughts, while on the feminine side mother nature makes sure that what has been decided comes alive into existence, thereby being created. This same relationship exists within our hearts and minds, the heart being the feminine and the mind being the masculine energy.

Let us also explore the duality of what I call the children or offspring of the heart and mind, created in the transition from the Spiritual to thoughts and feelings, then to energy and then manifestation into physicality and

mater, material substance. The relationship between the spiritual and physical, from spiritual to physical and back to the spiritual starts the cycle all again. The physical is the side of the coin vibrating lower so it appears more viscous and visible to the eyes, while the other side is vibrating much faster so cannot be seen by physical means. In terms of the physical, we can even trace duality all the way to the breath, the yin and yang of breathing in and breathing out being the most important physical means for life to be here, a process within which one discards the waste products and the other replenishes. The cycle of life lies in experiencing various degrees of these dualities and experiences, which within the process of creation, is an enriched form of observation and creates another duality in itself, experience and creation. The creator becomes the creating, creation and vice versa, as it is one and the same, happening within itself.

The "One" is the source, the God, the absolute constant. It contains the "All", everything in existence. So, the "One" is in all things and its universal laws or characteristics are also embedded in all things because, at the end of the day, all things emanate from it and stay within it. There can be nothing outside of it, as it is "All that is". All is in the One and the One is in the All.

"The One" stays within unconditional love at all times as it is complete and has the everlasting call of uniting "The All" as its children. While "The All" is formed through conditioning, the love energy is distributed into unique individual energies to simulate the illusion of separation and for individuality to be experienced as reality.

There is a relationship of duality between the constant absolute truest reality, which never changes, that of "The One" and the relative reality, which is temporary and has to keep changing for the purpose of experience and the vigor of life, that of "The All".

Anything that stays the same, never changes, and exists eternally, is infinite and complete in nature and is more of a truth than those with beginnings and endings or that which temporarily exists, such as fleeting memories or dreams to be experienced.

The highest duality of existence is the relationship between "God" as the constant, absolute and permanent reality and his dreams, imaginations, illusions or creations, which are temporary realities that we experience as real.

ELEVEN

BETRAYAL, JEALOUSY AND ATTACHMENT

Dream Memories 3rd August 2015

On the same night, I had a second dream, which is really about betrayals, jealousy and my attachments to others, to explore how I still handle such situations.

I would like to thank the energies of all my high school friends that played a part as characters in this dream.

I always love it when a dream starts with me living life. While partying and club hopping from place to place, I finally settled in one familiar club that I knew too well. I had done many events there, had helped to promote the club, and had even known the past owners and the new owners, now that the club has a different name. I was sort of like a VIP in the club but sometimes wasn't noticed depending on whom I met at the entrance or who was on duty in the club, and I always preferred to show up unannounced. Come to think of it, I've had so much history in the club that I even know the shapes and turns of the surrounding area.

I am amazed about this as this club does not exist in my awake physical reality, it only seems to show up in my dreams.

Moving around the club I started seeing very familiar faces from my childhood high school that have traveled very far from other countries just to be there, and it seemed like there was some sort of reunion going on. As opposed to feeling deprived that I could not remember being invited or told somehow, instead I felt the opposite, kind of more fulfilled for the night and very lucky to have stumbled on all these familiar faces from the past. It brought me so much joy to reconnect with these old souls. What are the odds that they are doing this in the country I reside in and in my favourite club, I said.

Everything was merriment until I saw him and I could not believe my eyes but there he was, with his brother and another close friend of ours. Then a strong feeling of betrayal immediately flooded my whole body. What is he doing here and how come he did not let me know this was happening? I asked myself as I saw him through the corner of my eyes. He was hiding, sneaking underneath a table, dragging his brother with him. It was just months ago when we organised a visa for him to come to visit my family and me here in Ireland, but he was not able to make it due to some unforeseen reasons and circumstances. But now he's here, probably with the same visa we organised for him and he has not told us anything about this.

He is a very loved childhood high school friend that I stayed close to over the years. We lived together in the same country, the UK, once before and I consider him to be still my "right hand man".

I felt quite shocked and the feeling of deceit and betrayal passed through my system for a few moments, which only lasted for a few seconds, yet it felt like an eternity. Until it settled as the memory of how much he was dear to my heart and how much I loved him started to creep in as I saw him cowering underneath the table, filled with guilt and regret that he had been caught.

This stood as a huge test for me and one I recognised very quickly after having had many practices, emotionally speaking. It was indeed an opportunity for me to apply all the knowledge and wisdom I have acquired so far about the choice of emotions, and that we have the power to consciously choose and change our emotions. Also that we have the power to detach from anything external with the deep knowledge that only the internal self is real.

I knew very well not to take any actions until I moved back into the desired feeling I preferred and also that my deep core base emotion was love for everything/circumstances, with no exceptions.

So I waited and allowed the feelings of betrayal to pass by and for the momentum to settle as I exercised slow, steady and long deep breaths, revitalising my whole system again until I gained enough space to intend the core love again.

But after a while, I received a backlash and a feeling of attachment came through, which did not feel that good to me. It was as if I possessed and owned this being because of the great attachment and expectations within the type of love I had for them. I noticed quickly that even though this type of human love was a wonderful type of love, it was not enough for my evolution, as it was not unconditional. In other words, conditions had to be met; otherwise, it would not feel good.

I strongly believe that I am everything and can not truly be separated from anything. Due to this truth, I do not need to own anything but to truly love every part of me, which is everything in existence and even nonexistence.

Everyone is completely free to do whatever they like. They do not need to take any permissions from me, because I no longer support the energy of master and slave.

All these realizations happened in a few seconds and it allowed me to be totally free of the situation, whereby from my love, it moved to comedy and laughter as I pointed at my friend underneath the table. I was amazed and very proud of myself for reaching this point so quickly and before engaging with my friend, feeling the transmutation of these energies to be where I wanted to be. I joined my friends and we merrily went around while he explained how it happened that he was there without my knowing.

We have talked about the attachments and betrayal that formed tests for me. Now the last part of the dream concerns jealousy towards myself and how I relate to it or how this affects me. It appeared that there was only one sponsor of the overall event, and this person paid for all to fly out to the event, paid for the club, accommodation etc. The sponsor was also one of my high school friends, and was highly respected on this day as everyone was very appreciative due to the amount of money he had spent to make this happen. They looked at him as practically the catalyst for all this joy and merriment.

My right hand man explained on a sour note that when he was approached about the event, and confirmed they were planning to do this in the country I resided in, he immediately told them he would get me on board. Before he could go on about the fact that he was meant to come visit me in this same country that year and this was where I resided, he was stopped by the sponsor of the event who expressed that he particularly did not want to see me there as he did not resonate with me or like me. He felt I was too full of myself and would end up having diva demands since I was considered a celebrity. He did not want to deal with this complication.

My right hand man did his best to persuade him, advising that, in fact, I was quite the opposite and he would really enjoy my company but this was to no avail. He even went ahead and questioned him about the other celebrities he had invited, "who ended up not making the event", but he answered that he knew them personally and was very ok with them.

My right hand man decided to say nothing until he got to the country I was in, then he would reveal this to me as a surprise, but it all backfired because as soon as they got here, they went straight to the club which was also their place of accommodation and there I was, getting to the surprise earlier than planned.

The true story behind the sponsor is that we were both very best friends in high school, even closer than me and my right hand man. But after high school, the friendship sort of drifted away and we never crossed paths again. I then left Africa, where we all grew up and I was seen as doing quite well, while he saw himself as suffering at that time, with no one coming to his aid. I remember a time he tried reaching out to me from Africa, but the conversation did not really go anywhere because, at this point, I was still busy struggling to make ends meet in a foreign land, while the people back home thought that the money grew on trees once you are abroad. This is due to many Africans abroad saving and piling up money to take back home so they can spend it senselessly for bragging rights about their achievements and for the status of being seen by society as someone wealthy and successful. This is a type of belief system that encourages stagnation within the evolution of the Africans who practice this. In a way, social conditioning becomes their master upon which everything in their life depends, so they remain slaves to the third density matrix.

Eventually, he also found his way outside the country and became very successful. I stumbled upon his number while I visited the country he was in and called him with so much excitement but did not receive the same from him. He was more concerned about letting me know how rich he had now become. I continued to call him, hoping to meet up and reconnect to enjoy our childhood memories but got no response from him, so I did not manage to see him before I left the country.

I do remember him saying on the phone, "so you are a celebrity now, huh?", and I could sense his unhappiness. It sounded like he felt I was one step ahead of him, while he really wanted to beat me at whatever game he felt he was playing with me.

The moment came and he finally spotted me at the reunion. He did his best for me not to be kept in. He walked straight up to me, addressed me and advised that I did not have the invitation to be there at the party.

This was a peak moment and a very sour note for me and for everyone else at the party. I knew that it was time again for me to pull in all the knowledge and wisdom I had to ride this type of situation, what one can call being in 'the eye of the storm'.

Everyone at the party wanted me to be there and was very happy to see me there. It was indeed a very big test for my ego/physical psychological consciousness, as a sense of acknowledgement started to come to me. It was like everything had started to fall on me. Some of our classmates went to negotiate with him but he became very furious, directing his bodyguards towards me. At this point, I did exactly what I normally would do in situations like this, I just stayed still with a smiley smirk on my face and without moving an inch, I then had the head space to glance my eyes around the club, looking at some of the staff members and then gaining the full acknowledgement that I actually owned fifty percent of the club and that this was only known by the few or higher level staff.

My psychological ego really wanted to pour down and rain on him as I saw that I definitely did have the upper hand, but I was quickly reminded and knew that I was no longer the type of being to go into a battle. I knew immediately that I had to release this energy. Still standing on one spot, now closing my eyes to take a few deep breaths, I was then able to re-introduce the feeling of love that I am, and went straight to him apologizing for any wrongs I must have caused him and asking if we could start all over again.

But this only escalated his fury whereby he brought out two knives and lashed at me, stabbing me underneath my heart but I did not feel a thing. The knife stayed stuck there as I moved towards him using my right hand to defend myself and trying to take the other knife from him. Then more people with security came to apprehend him.

My psychological ego/physical self was not too happy with me because it felt that we could have fought him back more physically or even taught him a lesson. I consoled my ego/physical self and looked down at the knife, pulled it out and magically. There was no blood and no hole to show I was stabbed and there was no pain felt either. I smiled and told my ego/physical self that he (ego self) would always be untouchable, protected and invisible to the likes of danger as he resonates and radiates higher vibrational and unconditional love, the power of the mind and spirit is proportionately higher than the physical. So, if you sort out your thoughts, feelings and vibrations, you most likely will never need to have physical battles etc., unless you choose to.

TWELVE

GUILT

Dream Memories 6th August 2015

I went to bed really late and had only two hours left to sleep. I closed my eyes and from the darkness, I floated into a dream where everything was dark. I could sense where I was and that I was in my childhood neighbourhood near a wasteland marsh area opposite the estate. I felt I was still in the air floating and about to land but I decided to land in front. I was still in the darkness but had no fear, even though this used to be a scary place for me growing up.

There were snakes, alligators and even wild dogs or wolves lurking around the bushes and marsh. I understood everything as part of me and with blind faith, I landed and started walking forward. A very heavenly sensation caught me, and I then used my physical eyes and saw that they had been closed all the while. It was so magical and enjoyable that I sped straight home to get to my wife and kid so they could experience this. I took them to a place that was like a club, with the help of a lady who was part of a collective. This collective felt like angels as they radiated such immense love, joy and serenity.

The atmosphere was so merry as she took them into the club and I lost them. I went on enjoying myself and planned to meet up with them later. After I had enough, I looked for them within the packed club until someone told me they were now looking for me and had walked to the bus stop. I was riddled with guilt because I had driven them there without the stroller, and now she had to walk all this way while carrying the baby in her hand. Knowing that she had not done this before and would blame me for her sufferings. I came to the awareness that I should not feel this guilt but kept conflicting and debating with my higher self about why I felt this, as I was still finding a resolution to my emotional state. I moved to the song from the club that was so enjoyable and kept playing in my head. I had noted this song and realized it was for me to record it down, for me to write in the future but I kept trying to record with my phone while in the dream and was not successful … I kept trying and woke up. Finally, in my awake state, I smiled and got my phone to record this song…

This dream, though, was to check and see that I had released my fears of wild animals and other sentient beings, which then allowed me to enjoy a larger portion of my heaven on earth. However, it extended itself for me to look more into the energy of guilt so as to transcend this into light also. Right before I went to bed I looked at my phone and saw a message from my sister asking if I could pick up her, my nephew & niece from the airport. They were meant to arrive in two hours. The feeling of guilt rushed through my whole body. I knew I had to sleep for the 1st part, that secondly, this meant I would have to only sleep one hour, which although I could do that, would have been very unfair to my physical body to ask it to drive to the airport knowing how in need of rest it felt. Finally, in two hours, my baby boy would wake up and I would have to mind him. I could do this with one eye open as long as I was there feeding him and seeing what he wanted to do in the morning.

At first, I was disappointed t because I would have loved picking up my nephew and niece after they had had a wonderful time in Canada, which had also contributed to their own evolution. I would have loved to welcome them with a wonderful energy of support so they could continue to grow and evolve in a much more positive way. The guilt crept in as I felt I was letting all of them down but the choices I faced and after going through all the reasoning, I eventually accepted that they and only they were totally responsible for their own fate. This understanding and realization put my attention back to divine light. And this was the wonderful dream that arose to mimic and explore more of the energies of guilt, in order to be released.

THIRTEEN

THE VOYAGE

Love of Self Towards Others

Dream Memories 9th August 2015

As I woke up from the first dream, I stayed within that vibration to absorb the memories from that dream as much as I could, and also the lessons of what that meant to me, after chuckling and being satisfied, I drifted into another dream. This dream also started as if we were in a schoolyard setting, sometimes there were characters that I recognised and sometimes I had classes upon classes to take.

I remember going around with my bag, which I held close to me as very important, finding my way navigating within this new school that was very massive, and making friends and acquaintances that were willing to help as I went along. Each time I would go towards a place that felt more like home, only because it was a place where my mother resided. It was the highest flat on a block of 8 flats and even though it had steps to reach there, I often floated up to go and see her and how she was doing, incorporating and integrating her lessons for the benefit of her own life. In the beginning, I was a bit concerned and I made sure to visit her more and assist with her learning. I also had, not all, but some of my siblings living in and around her, coming in and out to do the same thing. We would often learn from each other before going back into the main school for different classes. It was indeed a very massive schooling system.

It got to a point where I saw that my mother had it all figured out for herself and I did not have to visit her to help with this anymore. I felt much more settled about her and interacted with my siblings with more joy and relaxation. I decided to return back to the school that I saw as my main reason to be in that reality, but as I was journeying there I sensed that things had changed greatly, and I found it more difficult to find my sense of direction. Most classes were now filled with a much younger set of pupils and my set, which was a senior set, seemed to be finding their way out of the school.

I kept wandering aimlessly around the school, but I was looking for my sense of direction as if to know what to do next. I was not yet ready for school to be over. I had spent so much time teaching and helping my mum that I missed some classes. I really wanted to attend and intended to find these classes still, as I went around asking people and seeing most of my set going home and saying they would see me in the next school season.

This signifies and confirms to me that it is always best to finish attending to yourself within your life path before going out to help others, as it is the best and fullest way to help others. You want your cup to be full firstly and as it overflows, this overabundance starts to help others around you. Like the flight attendant saying, "Parents make sure to wear your own mask first before attending to placing them on your children in the case of an emergency". The belief is that every being is a sovereign being and will eventually find their own way, just like my mother had done. However, I was still very happy to help in any way, out of blind love even though the original contract was for me to fully help on a 100% basis after my own cup was full, as only then would I be giving the best of myself.

All this was also significant with what was going on within my awake state reality in terms of my immediate family and friends.

I realized it was time for me to go home and then the whole dynamics of the dream changed. Home became the place in the world I had really called home and not the home where my mother was within the school premises. I totally forgot that that existed and ventured to find my way home, while keeping my eye on my bag not to leave this behind anywhere and set forth on a journey to find home. I then, after much wandering, navigated myself outside the school premises and at some point realized I had left my bag somewhere, because each time I would meet new or old friends and we would play whatever it was that excited us, such as hide and seek, soccer etc. I traced my steps back to find my bag and kept asking many people questions so I could find the way to get home, and at some point, I realized that I was actually lost.

I was in a crowded city that looked like London city but it was very difficult to navigate my way or know how to get from a to b. The transportation system was much more difficult than usual. I kept going around in circles and eventually found some familiar spirits I could call family friends. They were twin brothers and I considered them my younger brothers. I was like a mentor to them growing up and they knew London city like the back of their hands, but this time they were not able to help me. It was as if they were mute and not willing to help or very unsure of what I wanted. I realized that they needed all their energy to find and help themselves and were on a one-way ticket home. I decided not to bother them and a thought came to my mind saying "*Follow them*" but I didn't even see any invitations from them. I quickly dismissed this thought because, after all, that was not what I really wanted to do.

I became a bit distraught and more weary because these younger ones I mentored at least knew their way home but I did not know my own way home. I made my peace with them and bid them farewell. I continued to track my way from the little information they gave and found myself more lost than ever. I tried to reach into my memory of the London city transport system, which I used to know by heart from living there in the past but found myself still wandering around. There was this sense of pride or shame in me at certain times that stopped me from asking a stranger, which could have helped to cut short most of the wandering. I got to a point of relief when I met a family member, a cousin that was actually going home and waiting to be picked up. I came to a sense of relaxation and joy in seeing her, explaining all the ordeal I had gone through and finally, it was all over. We continued to discuss and then I saw something very exciting across the street. It was someone or some being I really wanted to meet and there they were, right across the street from me. I gave my bag to my cousin and said, "*wait for me cause I will be back*".

When I finished meeting and discussing with this being I was full of excitement and joy but as I turned around to go back to my cousin, I found out that I was lost again. The whole reality had changed again. It seemed like this time I was now in a much noisier and crowded city, where others would consider it ten times more dangerous and rough than London city. The navigational system here was more than a nightmare. It was indeed Lagos city in the heart of West Africa, Nigeria, where I actually grew up in my younger years.

It was a familiar scene but one I had not faced for more than 15 years. As I was without my own backup security personnel that I once had in Lagos, this was a city I was most definitely not ready to be lost in.

I found myself within the very massive street markets and everybody was looking for something or opportunities to take from anyone who posed as a victim or looked like one. Many hungry faces and frowning faces, a sense of stress and frustration everywhere. The hustling and bustling with different types of loud noises, many kinds of funky smells attacking you from left right and center and even the air you breathe was not really air as it was laced with all types of pollution and dust. And the city's temperature was so hot that it did not help the situation.

It is a very large city, much bigger than London city, with overhead bridges, skyscrapers and very large and old vehicles that look very scary, as if they are not meant to be on the road but work perfectly as they move, adding to the noise and air pollution around.

Street hawkers and opportunists threaded around as this was the toughest spot within the survival of the fittest, arguments and fights breaking out here and there, drama everywhere.

Usually, when I visited these places, I was always at a safe distance within a safe and protected vehicle like the pope, but now here I am, lost in the middle of the whole chaos. I contemplated with myself and then settled down, realizing that I only had two choices, either to continue under a fear-based state of mind and perhaps end up a victim or to trust and become invisible, blending in with the scenarios to then find my way home. I chose to become invisible and blend in, bringing in an older version of myself who knew how to live and thrive in these types of situations.

I was also going against the odds of my previous beliefs. I will always stand out due to my coming from abroad and my skin not being as burnt as the natives, and my mannerisms would give away. I knew I was shining like a diamond within a bunch of black stones, but it didn't matter. This was going to be a test of my invisibility as *an untouchable*.

I realized I was noticed by everyone, but did not allow anyone to take any actions until I invited them, to ask them for help towards me navigating myself and in finding a trustworthy and commendable transportation system to get home. I walked in their midsts as if to be invisible and realized some went on with their normal day-to-day lives, not even caring about what I was about, while some got drawn to me and as soon as I could sense their negative intentions, I cut them off very quickly. As I now had a protective shield and was walking around without fear.

I then realized I had a lot of cash in my pockets and was quickly weary about this but stayed calm and still as if to put some protective energy into anything I felt was an opportunity for a mishap. I chose not to even bring my phone out, as I was doing my best not to attract any unwanted attention.

It then hit me, as I was now, in a way, part of the environment. I thought about my cousin, whom I told to wait for me with my bag. I knew they would have left because now a couple of hours had gone by. I kind of sent a message telepathically to advise that I would return home but it would be a long journey. I did not want to bother myself by thinking or harbouring any heavy feelings like worries and the likes, I was determined to stay positive on my path to get the best out of this journey.

I eventually started to see the beauty hidden and locked up within the chaos of such an environment as I walked around, being destitute who was finding his way home. Sometimes I would make friends with small families who had kids in this environment but were still finding a way to make a living. They found such happiness and joy within themselves, as they danced around listening to their favourite local music, living their very simple lives without any other worries. They explained to me or would often show me through their livelihood examples that yes, it is a concrete jungle out there, but once you stick to some codes and you know how to ride the wave, you have nothing else to worry about, and you can enjoy the best of life through nature's simplicity. (*This sent me a strong message and reminder of the great benefits of the simplicities of life*)

They would often welcome me in their little shops, which were also their homes, whenever I needed a place to sleep for the night. At this stage, I realized that days had passed.

I ended up developing a newfound envy for some of these people. I could see that their standard of living was very low as, according to my understanding, they had the most unfavourable conditions, but their quality of life was so profound and remarkable that they still had utmost vitality oozing out of them. Within the chaos, there was still much joy, high excitement and laughter. It felt like everywhere you turned there was a comedy show or some drama, and you did not need to turn on the television or pay for it.

They were also very close to nature, the animals and plants using natural things to heal and relieve themselves, and they were also highly creative and inventive. It was as if they could make anything out of nothing but did not have the right support or opportunity to do this on a massive scale.

After seeing and learning a lot from the sweetness hidden within this environment, even seeing violence in the streets and then the others showing togetherness and love for each other as they attended to their street matters, helping each other out within the chaotic environment, I decided that it was time for me to make that journey home and end this very educational voyage. I continued to wander and decided to venture into places I was not ready for, due to my not being ready to face the fears I had or thought I still had.

As I wandered around, I found myself stuck with a carnival of people near a beach. There was so much going on, and I kept walking around asking people for directions. Life was very easy to end for some and there were so many atrocities to see, but I turned a blind eye because I felt I had to focus and stay positive in order to get home, as opposed to being stuck with a heavy heart.

I was walking around the crowd and found myself on a sand hill facing the beach waters where all the locals set up their human shop, selling whatever you needed. I kept asking for directions, some gave me the wrong directions, while some totally ignored me. At the back of the hill was some manmade stream with fishes in it and green algae plants everywhere, and I somehow found myself stuck on a thin and long pavement by a wall behind the hill and water. Then it started raining and I realized my choice was to either work on the thin pavement supported by a wall with electric wires overhead or dive into the dirty stream water, which was also quite deep. I knew this was a test of my faith to see if I would choose the fear and create disaster or else create something more peaceful. I then thought of myself as a daredevil and walked on the thin pavement hanging onto the electric wires when I needed to. I knew I was perfectly safe.

At this point, I started getting an understanding of their public transport system and was ready to go on one of these machines, or should I say beasts, that looked like they should not be on the road. Then I got lucky and found someone who was meant to be a close friend.

He was with his family, so I knew they had a private ride. I believed I was now saved and begged them to help me out, but to my surprise, he expressed his hatred for me and refused. I spoke to his mother, who advised she had nothing against me and that she had always enjoyed the company of my mother. I must say she had always been a funny character as she told a joke and made me laugh. We were somewhere on an untarred street near the open gutters as they passed to and fro on a narrow wooden bridge carrying belongings and things they bought from the street traders selling local delicacies by the gutters. She continued that it was her son's car and she could not do anything about it. They disappeared and there I was, roaming again.

As I went to the major streets where I got to the bus stops, I met a young lady who looked pretty clean and trustworthy. She was with two of her younger brothers, I asked for help and she, too, said no. At this point, I looked suspicious and a little bit dirty, so she did not trust me.

I eventually met another slimmer older lady who also looked clean and even had an escort with her. She looked at me straight and said, "*You are lost, follow me and I will take you home, I will help you*". I was so full of joy and wanted to explain everything that had happened to me but she told me not to worry, as if she already knew all I had been through. So I followed her and her escort as we got to a bus stop and waited for a car to pick us up. She was quite a strange lady, who resonated very high vibrations, and high in spirit or should I say spiritual, but she kept picking up things from the ground, as if she was cleaning parts of the street. Her escort said nothing at all and just stayed there, sort of like a bodyguard. At one point, I felt the need to help her pick up and claim things, but the escort looked at me and said, "No" waving his hand as if to say I should leave her be. This was the only time he spoke or made a facial expression.

I felt safe anyway, and at this point, I realized I had a phone and decided to call my mother to let her know that I was safe and coming home. I told her about the good Samaritan and envisioned two elegant black cars parked in front of us. The fear struck again and made me think, "*what if they kidnap me?*" but this was dismissed very quickly. Yet this was now quite irrelevant as I now knew it was the end of the journey and I had already made it on one of the toughest streets as an untouchable. The dream ended with the feeling of me being home, and then I woke up.

This dream tested me on my fears and showed me in detail the lack of fear yet weariness within my physical mind and still in my vibration, "I could have simply stayed in one place with no concerns or wandering actions to take for me to get home. I could have just gone lucid in the dream and changed the reality that I was home already with a snap of a finger, but this would have defeated the purpose of the journey of physicality". It also tested the best of my faith and showed me the strong trust I had in my spiritual self, knowing that I am always and will always be taken care of at the end of the day. It also displayed some characteristics that I would have considered family or close friends, that I had close ties and attachments with, and who I believed would help me in critical times of need and could save me from weary situations, some might see as life-threatening. But they turned their back due to some not being strong enough to see and help anyone else.

I had to find out that the ones that really helped me were those I deemed as strangers or good Samaritans I had never met. This brought me to the knowledge that, only with the help of anyone within my reality, could I get to where I wanted to be. We are all one family, after all, so anybody can be in a position to help in the same way as a family should.

FOURTEEN

RECEIVING CREATIVE INFORMATION FROM DREAMS

Dream Memories 10th August 2015

In this dream, I saw myself with my cousin and friends. One of them was a music friend, and we were in what was like a hotel and club that they managed.

I had many fun memories of my cousin's friends slagging him about how he managed the place.

We then moved to the club section where my uncle was, around a VIP area. He was so happy to see me, and we discussed a bit about life and how I was getting on.

Then my younger cousin came in with a bunch of young friends and supporters. I saw they were getting prepared for performances. Then The club got filled up and she started performing. It was a very catchy song and I was so glad I waited because I had been about to go, not knowing this would happen.

Before other people started performing, I approached my younger cousin as I was so proud of what she had created and performed. She was happy too but a little disappointed because her dad read out the report from the royalties she made from the song and this was a bit small, so I advised her it was just the beginning and much more would come from the sales of the song, like endorsements and paid performances. They considered me an old head already in the game who knew about such systems. I was also looking at how they got their royalties and how to register my own songs with this aspect. My cousin was also leaving, so I advised her we must meet up later and discuss. She told me she was travelling with the family to Spain and would be back in three months.

I made my peace and bid her farewell, then continued to leave. I parked my car very close to the place, but I somehow forgot I had brought a car and so I started walking. It was apparent to me that I allowed myself to hold in my pocket some kind of drug some people were using, even though this was not my forte, and I never used drugs. I remember a policeman in the club looking for such drugs, and this got me weary and I looked for where and how to throw this away.... I started walking and the chorus of the song kept playing in my head as I navigated the streets to get back home. I did not want to meet any policeman until I ditched the evidence, this was me being wary about my stereotypical look that could sometimes provoke a stop and search, but I managed to control this by not appearing to be suspicious.

Even a passerby who had just from the club was also singing the chorus out loud because it got stuck in their mind. I became more proud of my younger cousin because, to my understanding, it was a very good song. Then I realized I had actually brought my car, which was parked very close to the club, so I had to get back there.

On the street, a lady was talking to a man as if they had just had a misunderstanding. She walked away talking to herself saying it was her fault for thinking she could find a good man from that part of the street. She herself did not look convincing as a good woman, she turned to the next guy and asked a few questions as if to see if they could hang out together and he muttered some words to her but she kept saying no. Even though he tried his best to sweet talk her, she just kept refusing and in my judgement, he looked more like a very decent person in comparison with her, as she was more abusive and street like. I kept walking back and realized I had to ditch the evidence because I was now going to pass close to the police station. I then ditched the evidence and the song kept building up in my mind. The words started coming into place as I walked joyfully to my car.

I then woke up and realized it was all a dream and I had received this song to record, work on and create. It was not a song that I had ever heard so it was a very new creation. I went straight to my phone and sang the song, recording it with joy as this was for me to do. I wondered and saw the way creation can be so effective once you are very free and willing to allow yourself to receive, and that it even comes so clearly from a dream state made so much sense.

Some of the stories in the dream ended up in the song as it fits in perfectly, and the song's place in the dream gave me more clarity about judgements and character.

FIFTEEN

UNDERSTANDING THE DARK LORDS

And Turning Darkness Into Light

Dream Memories 1ˢᵗ October 2015
Sicily-Siracusa Italy

In this dream, I existed within a beautiful and wonderful world where the people who lived here were so lovely, simple, beautiful and at peace with happiness. It was as if a divine bright white light encompassed and took care of the world. Until little by little, they started changing into darker characters, losing their pureness and going into more negative emotions like unhappiness, anger and hate, until it was as if they became like zombies who were only interested in infecting others.

I strongly felt as if I was the collective energy and spirit of these people, as I could feel every change and transformation going on. I later learned or noticed that I could even flow in and out of these people individually as if to say I was checking in on parts of my body to investigate and heal infected parts. Each time I would transform into one of the infected beings and heal that part of the collective, or sometimes I was able to heal a multitude of them at once, but this darkness and plague, as I may call it, grew stronger and stronger as it spread, driving the remaining people to move inwards and towards safe caves in the area.

Then an alien race appeared from nowhere, they had cat-like features but they were humanoid with very beautiful colourful faces. Oval shaped tattoos mixed with tribal markings were beautifully carved on their faces and they also had very big round eyes. At this point, the native beings in the world that my energy took care of were not consciously aware of me, but the alien race seemed to spot me easily and proceeded to come and have a conversation with me.

A feminine alien approached me. She was so beautiful and just wonderful to see and to be with. She had blue, grey and white patterns of stripes beautifully carved on her face. This alien race was filled with so much love and compassion that they had answered my call for help, so we continued to travel the whole world, healing those and the areas affected.

We got to the core of the darkness and realized cloaked beings, other alien races with dark intents who had infiltrated the world and continued to spread the darkness silently. We uncloaked them and drove them away until they got to a hiding place. With more of the catlike alien beings coming in with their spaceships and pumping divine light to terraform the planet/world and to uncloak all energies that were not meant to be there, we were able to discover that their hiding place was a very massive castle. This was where the darkness was being created and spread.

The other alien race, I will call the dark race, was led by an evil, dark and genius warlord who used the energies of newborn babies and committed the darkest known atrocities, without being noticed by anyone. I later learnt that this warlord and his race had already been driven away from another world. They had found my world and decided to sneak into it even though it was a protected area of purity due to the light and innocence of the people.

Once the warlord knew he had been discovered, he sent all his troops to come out in the open and attack in full force, wreaking havoc as they went by. The battle continued but the dark forces were no match for us, we aimed to protect the natives, infiltrate the dark forces and transmutate their energies into light energies. The warlord was genius enough to understand that we had already infiltrated most of his soldiers and the energy and spirit of that land and were now with him within his hidden castle that we had brought into our light. He quickly prompted me to negotiate and decided to show me fully his side of the story. He led me to different sectors of the castle, showing me all the atrocities they loved to take part in, and this felt very natural to them. He explained to me that this is how they have been created, to tend to the darkness within the light and dark polarity, saying this is what feels natural to them. He could see my love for all things, even himself, as I was a neutral and unconditionally loving being. He strongly hoped to sway me into giving them a place to exist in my world. I decided to go through all his secrets within the castle, as I saw this as an education for me to be without a bias, and so I could carry out a neutral judgment of equity where everyone wins, because we are all divine parts of the same neutral central source, and it does not matter whether we choose to live positively or negatively within a polarised reality.

This tour and experience of the dark castle then gave me the wisdom and power to re-educate the warlord and advise him that his energy was an ancient energy that no longer fit or had a place in the new world they were in. However it could always be remembered as it was indeed a very important part of existence within the polarity of the worlds, and they were divinely created to serve those purposes but these purposes are now irrelevant because they are no longer in play. The evolution of the world has now moved on.

And so, with the help of the beautiful light alien cat looking race, we relocated the dark lord and his people to a different sector, within a different universe, where they can be left alone to practice their darkness on each other, until they choose not to reincarnate as these dark races.

In the world of unconditional love and neutrality, there's no place for the spread of evil. Evil should be only onto itself, until it implodes into neutrality and back to the love from which it was created. The darkness is only an illusion created from the absence of light, *light a candle in a dark room and the darkness goes into non-existence, same as if you put off the candle and the darkness comes back on.* So the light can be seen to be more real and can take precedence before the darkness, as most prefer the light side of this phenomenon, but both are actually the same coin, only just seen from the two different perspectives of polarity.

(My name was RAY: I was the entity, the soul and the protector of this beautiful world in my dream)

SIXTEEN

DREAM AND AWAKE REALITY MERGE, CHANGE AND TRUST

Also Receiving Creative Information

Dream Memories 31st Jan 2016

I find myself in a dream outside a type of school or community complex, loitering in and around an open but roofed high platform assembly ground. There was an instrumental music beat going on, and I noticed I was with two other of my friends who were musicians as well, and we were co-writing a song and walking around gathering inspiration where we could. I was so much in my element and it felt so good. It had been so long since I wrote a rap song, so I was deeply immersed in the creative process of the lyrics as if it was part of my soul. With a paper and pen in my hand, I kept 'vibing' with the flow and throwing my emotions on the paper as I jotted down the lines, I could hear my friends also doing the same and we gave ourselves notations of corner pieces of the song. It was a very merry experience as I have missed doing this so much. I then got a little lucid in the dream, asking myself and checking if it was a dream, but it felt so real as I pressed my pen on the paper. I then shook the paper vigorously but I was more and still deep within the creative process. I was not quite sure of the part of my mind that asked if it was a dream at that moment, so I continued with the writing until I reached a block. Once there was this struggle in trying to channel the next line of information, I woke up and realized it was a dream but I still had a strong memory and feeling of the song. Also, I was a little disappointed that I had not written it on physical paper because I thought it was really good.

I quickly jumped out of bed and went to a different room with a pen and paper to jot down the lyrics, which I still remembered and continued to formulate the last line where I had the block. After all this was done, I retired and went back to sleep.

In this dream, I understood it was also communication between myself and my multidimensional higher spirit self that is always awake and observing all, whereby I was advised that we were fully back into the joy of our creative elements within music, to remind me of the ecstasy we feel when we create.

As I slept again, I was drawn into another dream where I do not remember all of what happened, up until a point where I found myself waiting or chilling in a restaurant with a couple of family and friends. I was not really sure what the occasion was but I remember going outside the restaurant to get some money out of a cash machine just in front of the establishment. As I brought out the cash from the machine, something very strange happened. The money note was a weird colour I had never seen, some sort of greenish blue and the amount on the note was not a round figure, it was exactly 78 euros, or so I thought, but it did not really say euros. I became perplexed and as the card came out of the machine, it also was not one of my familiar cards. I was not sure how it came into my possession and how I knew how to use it. I checked the receipt for more information but this confused me some more.

The staff members of the establishment and a family member were also with me, trying to resolve my confusion. After checking all my wallets and cards in my pockets, things got more confusing. We eventually gave up on the machine to go into the restaurant.

Everybody else was happy and content, apart from myself. I was happy about the fact that I only tried to take twenty euros and was given seventy-eight euros, or some sort of currency, that paid for all the family and friends. But I was not all that trusting and wanted to find out more.

While back in the establishment, everyone else was happy and having fun except for myself and a friend of mine was waiting for me to solve my riddle, but eventually, she started sleeping as this was taking too long. I mean, here I was, still battling the situation, taking everything out of my pockets, going through receipts, and finding out I had so many other cards but I was not able to find the original card I was used to. I later gained some trust that I was being taken care of somehow but I was bent on investigating and finding out who or what was taking care of me and where my original card was. My family at this time were enjoying themselves and passing me treats as the stewards came to serve around our tables, and then something extraordinary happened.

While still rambling through all my wallets, finding more cards in my pockets, my wife who was on my right-hand side and passing me a cheese treat, then turned into my sister. This was not one bit weird to me because it was as if my sister was the one there all along. My reality then shifted as if to split, whereby I bled into the awake reality in which I was actually still on the bed sleeping and my son had woken up beside myself and my wife. He was waking my wife up and making beautiful cute noises, but the thing is, at the same time, I was still sitting at the restaurant, determined to sort out their riddle, which bothered me until I could resolve it. I shifted back into the dream where I was sitting down and told my sister to hold on to the other treats and that my son was very cute and I would get to him as soon as I resolved this riddle. I was pointing in front of me as if I could see the awake reality on a screen. It was magnificent as I could feel both realities and be on both sides simultaneously. It was not until my son called out to me saying "Dada" that I realized that I could forget about this confusing place and that it was only an illusionary dream anyway. I felt a big weight lifted off my shoulders and had a sigh of relief as I realized that I didn't really lose my main card or anything, so I happily joined my son and wife back fully awake on the bed with his smiling face looking at me, laying next and giving me kisses.

1. *This dream showed me in depth how we, as humans, are very stubborn to change even if it is to bring about a positive situation. There is still a reluctant energy as if we are waiting for the penny to drop at any point. The card I was looking for did not even have up to that amount so it was pretty clear that I was being looked after by my multidimensional higher spirit self because I used a different card. I did not necessarily know where it came from and somehow was able to apply the pin code and get money out without problems.*

   But the lack of trust and the belief that we are not worth it or the fear of the unknown made me suspicious, as if it might be a trick so I had to be sure and watch out. Even when I gained this trust, I still wanted to understand how I got this help, and because I could not find my old familiar card, which was not even as good as the new one, I still felt uncomfortable due to this unfamiliarity.

2. *The second lesson I learnt was that I could always choose whichever feels better out of different realities set in front of me and that the previous or past reality no longer exists, even if it was just a moment ago. The only thing keeping me there was the unresolved issue and once this got resolved, I opted out and then entered the new reality. So the only thing that remains and exists is the current moment you have chosen and are focused on. This I felt as the relief came that I did not have to continue being uncomfortable looking for a card in my dream after choosing to wake up. Instead, I could choose to enjoy the awake reality where my dear loving son and his mother were waiting for me.*

MULTI-DIMENTIONAL

INTER-DIMENTIONAL

SEVENTEEN

THE HIDDEN DARKNESS WITHIN US

Dream Memories 1st February 2016

In this dream, I remember the end part where I got a valuable lesson, and was quite surprised about my reaction as I had always thought of myself as unconditionally loving in many aspects of my life, but this was a situation I had not been put in before. You never know what energies within you feed your reactions until you get tested with the right situations.

I had just finished working in a very high-profile radio station, having had an interview liaising and extending my connections within the music industry. I was on my way to another event where I met up with one of my sisters, who was at that time surrounded by so-called high-profile people from the music industry, including some I had already met at the previous spot. She was so excited and wanted to introduce me to them as she explained that she had gone to school with one of them.

As I was gathering my thoughts on approaching the group, I was putting on my business mind and professional hat and I spotted some other rather rough and shabby dangerous looking groups approaching, some of them even had some teeth missing and the like. It was outdoors and there seemed to be some kind of carnival happening with different calibers of people all around.

I was introduced by my sister and made my acquaintance as we continued with a business conversation. At this point, the rough and shabby-looking group had reached where we were and one of them shouted out my name with such joy and love that it was as if he knew me from somewhere, and he did. I am generally an all-round people person, whereby I attempt not to discriminate or judge. This is why people of all calibers had somewhat of a liking of me. They considered me very playful, cool and down-to-earth.

I remembered him as a Dj in a smaller local club just around the way, and he also had a gap in his mouth as a tooth was missing.

What I did next would haunt me afterwards and this is how I got to learn that valuable lesson. I quickly smiled at him, nodding my head and waving my hand for him to move past, saying, "Hey! How are you doing? I'll see you later".

It was as if I was telling him that I was in a very important meeting and I did not want him to disturb me and more so that I did not want to be seen with the likes of him, so I judged him because I felt that I would be judged by the so-called high profile music individuals and might miss future opportunities with them. He sensed I was not the same "Stone" he knew on the street or in the clubs and cordially moved accordingly. All this happened in a split second that I could not take back, and I later decided to explain and defend my reaction to myself within my head but it still did not feel right.

I woke up at this point and realized the energy that I had within the dream that caused me to react in such a way and a feeling of disappointment passed through me very swiftly. I asked myself a question, "What would Fela Anikulapo Kuti do if he was in the same situation?". Fela is one of the greatest music legends in Africa who created his own genre of music called "Afrobeat". He was at the pinnacle of my legend board while growing up. I adored him and always wanted to be like him.

Fela was an enlightened, wise being who had such great love for the ordinary people and did not let anything whatsoever come between them. His residence was seen as and called a shrine where every caliber of people came, not only to have fun but to even make a living. Fela was an international legend that toured the world and brought back the money to cater for the vast amount of ordinary Nigerians who lived in and around the shrine, as he saw that the government chose to ignore and enslave the less fortunate. Instead, he did not care for any material things or status, just his music and the empowerment of the people.

I quickly understood this and was very happy that I showed myself this energy and old patterns of belief systems that no longer served me. I became more appreciative and thankful that I had used the opportunity within my dreams to see more clearly and to have this energy released. I no longer will have to live through that in the awake reality because now I know what my heart would do better, from clarifying my true heart's desire after facing a situation like that. I now know that I will do my best to give the appropriate amount of care and respect to both parties. The one I was standing with and also the 'tooth gap party' who were passing by and saying hello to me.

EIGHTEEN

ANGER, IRRITATION AND WORRIES

Dream Memories December 2016
Back in Hawaii

When you analyse the details of dreams with your psychological ego/physical mind and stretch this with a bird's eye view of your higher mental mind, "The mind of the heart and spirit", you realise that whatever it is is not worth the trouble you assign to it.

It is not worth it for you to loiter in your creational vibration space (how you feel) with these little trinkets of unsettling energies, which makes you project and create a reality that is not really clear or not to the liking of your highest benefit.

I had been cleaning up my creative space, and drawn to focus on the little things in life that trigger a subconscious reaction embedded in my ARS "automatic response system" and to make sure that these responses adhere to my highest benefit. Otherwise, I would work on re-writing these programmes.

The programme of how we react to money is a very big one for me. I have attached so many belief systems to this, and I was giving myself opportunistic scenarios to see how I would react and change this pattern as time went on.

I'm finally reaching the end of deep beliefs that had helped me sustain a poor man's mentality, as they call it.

ANGER, IRRITATION AND WORRIES

A transformation happened regarding the irritation of how much money one is spending versus the joy and immediacy of the safety net that is felt when one receives a substantial amount of money.

As I woke up at seven AM sharp on my second trip to the sacred land in Hawaii, Maui, I recollected final messages and memories of my dream, which was actually about a completely different subject, that of "Anger and Revenge".

I was also shown clarity of how irrelevant little worries associated with the money spent did not make any sense at all to keep harbouring, and I finally released these worries and let them go.

I got a text message from my Irish phone number, which I was using and roaming in America, and it caused the unsettling energy of the thought, "I am roaming with my phone, and this is really costing me". So I had to look at this with the mind and truly understand what the energy was about and why something in me felt it had to hold on to such bothersome feelings.

I needed to shed some light into this darkness, so I simply just counted the text messages I had received since I arrived, and stipulated or estimated how much more there would be, if any more, for the rest of my trip. I could clearly see that this did not amount to anything, or come close to anything that warranted any reason for me to continue holding on to such disruptive creational energies or "Worries" that did not serve my highest benefit.

So I felt myself breathe in and out in a very calm and relaxing way as I finally let go and released these energies.

I also understood that I would have final dreams to see myself not being triggered by this energy anymore and would have lots of opportunities to see this in the awake reality also.

When I first landed in the USA, I proceeded to change my currency from Euros to Dollars and had an opportunity to be bothered and not happy because, after the change, I was left with only seventy-five percent of what I brought in due to some charges. When I was doing the currency exchange, a thought quickly sped through my mind saying, "you should have...".

But it stopped mid-way because I have done well to reprogram my Automatic response system to know the past and future as irrelevant unless desired information is needed in the NOW. And also to be aware and recognise what thought or feeling I am allowing to fester in me.

For example, "I should have done my currency changes in Ireland" was like spilt milk and there was no need to dwell on or waste any energy on that type of thought.

The next thought still silently crept in to say, "The money you have is not enough for your trip and you may fall into difficulties. You better start seeing how to get more money". It felt like I had been practising my evolution over the years for just this moment.

I did not believe this voice in me one bit. I knew it was a lie because I had grown to know and trust other higher aspects of myself, "My spirit guides, angels, and what I call my higher self or higher consciousness" that I was working with, and I knew they were the sponsors for this trip, so there was nothing for my physical mind to worry about.

Instead, I will do nothing and just move on with the notion that it will be perfect and magical. ALL WILL BE WELL.

After I had acknowledged and purged the poor man's mentality, coming from the energies within me that created doubts and the false illusion that things were not ok, for me to now buy into this again and continue to create old paradigms of survival and suffering through my old belief system, would be detrimental to my growth.

Since I am now very clear and have a full understanding of my choices, resting my vibration with the feeling of relief, comfort and the great sense of being taken care of, there was no need for any such worries anymore.

The result and outcome of the above decision astonished me deeply.

At this point, I had already spent many days in Maui, with only two days left before returning to Ireland, and I also do remember spending a considerable amount of money without checking or calculating what I had left. I did not create a budget or come up with any plans on how to spend the money I had as I felt really free, and also knew I was being taken care of spiritually.

The shock I experienced when I counted how much I had left was incredible.

It was such a huge surprise because it was exactly the same amount I had collected from the currency exchange office when I first landed some days prior.

This was a momentous event for me and I did my very best to explain it to myself but to no avail. I kept doing calculations of what I had spent but could not figure it out. The only thing I could think of was, "This is magic". How could I have spent money for the trip and at the end of the trip still have the exact amount I came in with? I was really baffled and struck by how a refreshed and positive belief system can truly create miracles. Now here I am with so much money, all because of what I strictly chose to believe.

Now back to the dream before this one, in which I was working on the emotions, "Anger and revenge" and fine-tuning to release the aspects that did not serve my highest benefit and then turning this into a neutralizing of my passion, fire and will. The innermost power of my masculine energies.

I am in this dream as a very successful club owner, with officials, like the Men In Black. Everything was going really great till another billionaire character arrived. I provided everything for him as I was his host, and showed him around the business and the city as he was very interested in this.

He got very comfortable and spent a considerable amount of time within my establishment and at this time, I was quite busy flying in and out with my chopper or private jet, but I would still see him here and there.

Then it happened, I came one day to my club and everything felt strange. It seemed everything had been taken over by him. Then the billionaire and his people, including the security agents, came up to me and issued a warrant for me to be out of the property, with some legal papers stating that it was now owned by him.

This was a huge event for me but even though I was in a dream, I knew all the inner work I had done and knew there was no need to panic and this was an experience I had called on to myself. So the question of "why" was the loudest at that point.

I did my best to keep my cool but I needed this sorted out asap, and there were two prominent feelings strongly begging me to choose them and react.

I was angry that this could happen and that I just lost my estate like that. All I worked for? It moved me into victimisation. I knew that if I took on board these feelings, I would be giving my power away as a victim who now needs help from the outside, so I stayed strong and trusted that there would be a higher resolution and if this was just for me to let go of material things, then this was the biggest lesson of them all.

I was allowed to come into the premises and take my crew there every day to spend money, have fun and see how all transpires with this new change. The fight in me was not that prevalent but the feelings kept coming up to the surface for me to use them, and each time I accepted the situation and allowed the feelings to be released and recycled by the planet using my deep breathing techniques that I am very skilled at.

But the feeling of revenge was the trickiest to deal with. Before I knew it, my mind would slip into some strategic plan to revenge as it would feel really good, but I stayed strong to see it as a trap because I knew it would only feel good temporarily. My mind compelled me with wonderful genius schemes of revenge, which I went through and made peace with until one day, I dropped from my chopper and left it hovering above while I joined the party in the club just to quickly see what was happening.

This was when I saw the billionaire again with his entourage and lawyers rushing to let me know that my wife has now been taken from me also, that she had left me to go to him, and then I saw my wife at his back to confirm this.

I can only describe the feeling after I asked, "How is this even possible?" All the revenge voices in my mind saying, "I told you so" put me in a frenzied kind of emotion where I just took direct actions. I found myself back in my chopper, flying with something tied with a rope dangling below.

Even though I was not too proud of my actions, it gave me a sort of temporary relief. I laughed as I saw myself flying away from the dream and getting more lucid and conscious, asking myself, "So that is what you will do?". This gave me a great understanding of why some people go rogue and become zealots as they are so impacted that they can not see any other choices than to react to the powerful emotions consuming them.

I felt great relief that it was just a dream as I slipped back into the awake world. What a very testing dream I said, "I had just enacted the 'What would you do?' scenario".

So on waking up, I got the roaming text message which then led me to the realization.

NINETEEN

GENERALITY OF DREAMS AND SPIRITUAL CLEANSING WORK

With Sacred Crystals Within Dreams

Dream Memories 23rd December 2019
Spain 'Ronda, Malaga'

The contents of dreams generally concern thoughts or deep thoughts or experiences within the awake reality whereby the subconscious/unconscious spirit mind now feels the need to extend this into the dream worlds to continue exploring more options if the overall being feels not enough was explored during the awake reality.

Before sleeping, I was getting in tune with current political affairs around the world and so many ideas and analyses were going through my psyche and energetic space. There was intrigue from a particular world leader who was really shaking the tree of world politics. He was quite interesting to watch and everyone wanted to know what he would do next. There were many negative actions and reactions but in summing it up on a positive note, so many world issues had to be exposed to the surface to be dealt with by the energies of the human collective.

This had already been predicted after 2012 by certain spiritual communities I was privy to, that a certain wild card would be a major shaker and mover of issues non-beneficial to the human race and would be brought up to the surface for change, as it was understood that the human collective was due for an evolution of the way of being, whereby heavy and dark issues are looked at again and dropped for lighter and joyous or more peaceful and loving resolutions.

And the internet plays a huge part as an engine to unite all thoughts and choices towards new and more beneficial collective directives.

In the past, most energies and ideas were sectoral, staying in their individual communities and were not enough to impact the world at the rate at which the internet provides. Now large-scale communities are merged together by the internet and are being well informed of the happenings of the world through this set platform, whereby there has been an ongoing wealth of protests, unity and actions towards change.

As intriguing as this world leader's character was, my interest was so deep that I did not have enough time to process it in the awake reality, so it got dragged into my first dream.

I found myself side to side with this character in a leisure building where the very wealthy converged. I saw myself as a billionaire having deep conversations with this character, trying to understand his point of view and deciphering the positive benefits therein. After enough exploration here, I woke up and on going back to sleep, a different dream emerged.

This time there was yet another topic I had pondered on within my awake reality, a gathering with my high school alumni colleagues that I was going to miss physically but really wanted to be there. So I had the opportunity in my dream to explore and enjoy time spent on a version of how that gathering may turn out to be with my character in the mix, using my dreams as a land of exploration and experience.

Sometimes the generality of dreams can be so clear and directly powerful towards the opposite side that one has a dream and it spills out into the awake reality, whereby most of the same details now appear to be happening in real life awake reality, "most people refer to this as seeing a vision within the dream state that later comes to past within the awake reality".

I will give an example of one of my sister's dreams, in which she saw a black Mamba snake in my mother's house in Africa and when she woke up, she immediately called my mother who then confirmed that yes, the same snake was found at the back of her deep freezer and she raised the alarm for that to be taken care of.

There are no patterns of reasons why this happens. Sometimes, it serves as a warning or opportunity to prepare with precautions or sometimes, it is just to inform after the effect. Or we can even say it is due to a very powerful momentum of set topics and vibration. It could have a double spill in the dream and into the awake reality or vice versa. Such topics would have been saturated within the consciousness. This is sometimes due to core fear or a powerful love that takes up one's attention.

I woke up again after my second dream on the same night and slipped into a third dream. After that, I woke up again to go into a fourth dream.

Now, these two last dreams were somewhat unique types of dreams that I will do my best to explain. These dreams stem from my core belief systems about everything being energy vibrations whereby everything has its own unique frequencies, the same notions as Albert Einstein and Nikola Tesla.

I am part of spiritual communities that use healing frequencies to resolve and balance problematic energies around the world. This I do on a day to day basis using crystalline frequencies or just my innermost subtle and balanced healing vibrations.

Sometimes this part of my work is done within my dream state reality, as there may be less hindrance for the benefit of some unique situations.

I have been doing this all around the world and now concentrate in Africa, carrying my crystals around to neutralize problematic spots in the planet, for example, war or conflict-ridden areas, or even individuals who need cleansing and balancing, as they will be very beneficial to themselves and humanity at large, some have even reported the healing of physical and psychological ailments and such phenomena that I will not go into deeply in this book.

As the proprietor of this book is my multidimensional self, which includes a battalion of archangels, their intention is for this part of my dreams to be featured in this book.

The third dream was indeed the healing of individual energies, meeting these energies on a one-on-one basis and administering any healing patterns applicable to them, which in turn benefits these energies in real life awake reality. Some energies are able to realize this and then converge with me in the awake reality for more understandings, extensions and resolutions. *Sometimes this is somewhat magical, whereby I meet someone I helped work on the dream state, now face to face in the awake reality, they sense the familiarity with me, and after all is said and done, I let them know I had already met them and the work already started for them within my dream state.*

I will now skip to the fourth dream to demonstrate this. As I was in a vehicle on the way home in the streets of Lagos state Nigeria, we were passing by some side street market where they were selling delicacies and sweets I remember growing up with and dearly missed, as I have been out of the country for so many years. I decided to stop and patronise these market women who were all so enthusiastic about making a sale. As I stepped out of the car and started buying a few delicacies, I heard three market women to the right, drawing my attention towards them as if for me to come and patronise them.

As I was picking up and selecting the goods I wanted, I realized they were more interested in the healing crystals in my hands that I always carried to energetically help anyone I came in contact with. It was as if they knew that if I bought anything from them, their way would open up to more prosperity and more sales.

They were more concentrated on giving me so many free goods as if to say my patronage was more important than the sales. I realized that these were beings who understood the meaning of the crystals' energy work for them and were not intending to let this opportunity slip by. I looked into their eyes with utmost satisfaction and appreciation, as I saw their shining eyes glow with diving light, wisdom and understanding.

I felt very at home with these beings and decided to commence with a spiritual ritual of toning at the top of my voice to clear the paths and ways, neutralizing and balancing the energies in the market for more prosperity and goodwill.

Toning is the announcing and projection of frequency vibrational sounds through the voice to align the vibrations within the body or chakras of the body and also balance the frequencies and chakras of the outside environment.

Chakras are the different nodal energy points between the internal and external body and environments where different vibrational forces converge and unify towards the ONE body of consciousness that is all in existence.

TWENTY

THE POWER OF THE HUMAN CELLS

Dreams Memories 24th December 2019

Before I go into this dream (about the community of cells and my communication with a leader of warrior cells, cleaning up and fighting off any infections), I want to first give you an idea of the context and a premise of my belief system and knowledge, about the reality I have enjoyed due to this.

In 2009, I had a major physical illness which led to and triggered my path to enlightenment, self-realization or just human evolution, whatever name this process can be called. I decided I would no longer give importance or attention to what humans call harmful microorganisms that cause illnesses or other types of deformities in the cell or diseases. In fact, I decreed and considered them non-existence as I was deeply and greatly understanding that everything is just a beautiful and wonderful illusion. So I decided to only experience the positive side of this coin, and in turn, see anything in my reality as perfection with a hundred percent right to be there, which will always eventually end up being a positive benefit to my soul and others. After following and learning from many metaphysical, inspirational and spiritual teachers, I saw diseases as "Dis-ease". As in not being at ease within the physical body or mind, which originates from whatever is brewing in one's energies due to the thoughts, feelings, perceptions and beliefs one holds. Whereby because of these vibrational disturbances, the cells are in turmoil and operating in an opposite fashion, as opposed to the natural way.

I discovered that we could communicate with our cells and that we are made up of trillions of cells which arrange themselves as different communities connected together as one. I realised that these tiny little beings are very powerful and would continue to produce and create healthy life unless redirected by the psychological mind, which may be afflicted with limitations due to the emotion or energy of fear and the stipulation of survival within one's belief system.

This is due to the misuse of intellect given to humanity by consciousness. For example, other living things like wild animals, are instinctual without much intellect. It is quite straightforward for them as they blindly follow their instincts and continue with the natural way of things. Their sense of frequencies and vibrational changes are at the peak of a hundred percent, so they depend solely on this to navigate their world, which means they always have their internal guidance systems operating and no intellect to confuse them otherwise. It is true that they, too, sometimes experience the process of dis-ease, which is either resolved through their own remedies in nature or it is just a natural sign for them to leave the world. Otherwise, they need human intervention to stay alive.

I realised that for me to be in accordance with these superpowers called cells, I would need to align my mind towards their divine workings, stay with a positive belief system that recognizes their power, continue with life eternally and not ever try to contradict them. I will also need to support them with the best physical food materials and to keep them active somehow, exercise being a paramount means, so as not to send the wrong signals to them, such as that of a dis-eased situation or worse, the retirement and death of the overall community.

We can not look at death on its own because there is no true death since we are a mass of energy and energy never dies. It can only be transformed. Also, the overall consciousness continues and never ends because it never really started, "SPIRIT is eternal and Infinite".

Cells die and new ones are born every day, so "Death" is a pivotal part of life. The beginning of a story and the end happens in its own natural timing.

As I continued my day to day workings of life, having made a conscious decision to change my perspective on health, I realised that after about three years, I had not been physically unwell. I had not even had the common cold flu virus, which I always had almost every year in the past. But until my realisation, it was symptoms of this same virus that I was now feeling at this point that awoke my realisation. I looked at myself in the mirror with a stuffy nose and a bit of a cough, so I wondered and said to myself, "I seemed to have pulled this off for three years, but what have I done wrong now, that I have attracted this again?". I went back to my belief that everything within my reality was there for a beneficial purpose and there was no other way.

I decided to take it as a positive thing and it only lasted for three days. After this, I started getting strong signals within my inner guidance system that I should eat more healthy food and do more exercise, so I planned to change my ways. The only thing I had changed prior to this was my mindset with a conviction that only beneficial and helpful microorganisms would exist within my world.

Prior to this, I remember having deep conversations with my inner-self, which at that time I called my "Higher-self", that I would love to live up to my hundreds and still be and look very young and healthy. I was supported internally so this was very possible, but I will have to also take some external actions of changing my diet to a much more water based and healthy diet, and also exercise my physical body for the benefit of the cells. My internal spiritual senses I now call my Angels, at that time, advised me to meet them halfway.

I went into some sort of prayers and decreed that I would endeavour to do my best and if I was not successful by myself, then I would need their help.

After some years, a phenomenal incident happened, that changed my whole orientation of what and how I choose to consume food, and it marked my heightened sensitivity and how I had changed towards a healthy living and youthful looking orientation. I always enjoyed it when others commented I looked too young for my age, so I wanted to keep enjoying this as much as I could, so this was indeed a very huge blessing for me, but it came with a powerful force of experiences that knocked me down greatly and even also affected my loved ones around me.

I went for a holiday to London, UK, to assist my mother, who was there from Nigeria, for her medical checkups and the like. It was also the period of a very popular carnival called the Notting Hill West indies carnival. As a musician myself, this was a plus and something I was looking forward to.

I was meant to spend only three days there but I ended up spending more due to an unforeseen event that happened while I was enjoying the carnival, meeting friends from all over the world who travelled to also experience the carnival. At this point, the medical checkups with my mother had been accomplished and it was supposed to be my last day in London as I was meant to catch a late night flight back to Dublin, Ireland.

I found myself following a group of youthful and rugged looking people who seemed not to really care about me, and only one of them I sparsely knew, as he was a friend of a friend. They seemed to be wanting to distance themselves from me and at this point, I realized I was very intoxicated and staggering as I walked. It felt like a dream but it wasn't, and then I remembered I was supposed to be at the airport. I looked at the time and with the calculation of distance and transport, I knew I would not make it there in time, nor could I properly coordinate myself to make the journey. I stopped following these groups and found my way towards the subways, where I then sat down somewhere outside to think of what my next step was. I realised that this was no ordinary intoxication and it felt more as if I had been poisoned or drugged somehow from following the wrong crowd. I managed to get into a store and a pharmacy and managed to get some sort of help with medicinal fluids, which seemed to help me temporarily. I then thought of one of my very close friends who was like a brother to me, and I let him know my predicament. He advised me to stay where I was as he and his friends were on the way back to London from a different county and they would come and get me there in about two to three hours. I waited patiently and got a little bit better until they showed up.

It was a festive period and my friends were delighted to see me. Everyone was still in a party mood and it looked as if I was much better, so no one objected as I grabbed the huge bottle of cognac and continued with more intoxication. It was not something I could not handle in the past so we continued to party and got to a friend's house to book a different ticket for me to fly out the next day.

The next day came and it was almost as if I had not slept and was still on a high, thereby delaying my time to get to the airport and missing the flight again for the second time. At this time, my dear friend was out of options and frustrated, not knowing what to do as he now realized that all this while I had not been ok but only just elongated the merriment in me and did not seem to be getting sober but worse as I started not to make any sense, according to the onlookers, and it was as if I was completely out of this reality.

A third flight ticket had to be bought and he did his best to get me to my family in Ireland. Also, he knew he had to take me to where my mother was, which was really a last resort.

My memory drifts in and out of being in another friend's mother's house where my mother was and giving them a shock of their lives. They used to see me as the wonderful golden boy, but now I had become a beast and a demon joined together. They were very religious, so they kept praying and sprinkling holy water and anointing oil on me, and also there were so many bibles around me.

Eventually, I slept and woke up ok, but with no or very little energy. I became very sensitive to everything, light, loud noises, sporadic movements and even my taste buds became so sensitive that I could only drink water and eat very pure and virgin food in little quantities, mostly liquids.

It was while I was still in this very intensive state and when I got back home in Ireland that I re-discovered the water based food, the vegetable called 'Cucumbers', which was the only food my body allowed to stay in at first. Others were spat out or even too strong for my sense of smell or taste and I eventually vomited if I forced myself to eat them, due to their level of impurities.

There was a new authority and 'Sheriff' in town, which was the 'Intelligence' of my body which encompasses all the battalions and communities of powerful cells in our body moving in unison to speak as one and to temporarily overthrow the psychological conscious mind, which does not benefit the overall being.

Whatever the mind wanted, the body rejected, so I was forced to tap into a different kind of intelligence, whereby I would look at the food base in the shop and something chooses food I had never tried before, and once it entered my mouth, there is a feeling of revitalisation in nutrition, freshness, fulfilled and content, the most I tried were fruit and vegetables. This was a very new type of sensation for me. I never knew this type of sensation existed, and after practicing it for a while, I was now able to tell the difference between what my body wanted and needed versus what my psychological mind was looking to consume. Before that, I usually just ate whatever my mind wanted and sometimes this may not have been the best for the body, but if the body decides what to eat, it will then always pick the right and healthy option for itself. After nine years, cucumber remains a major staple in my meals even though I allow myself to indulge in whatever interests my mind or body, as long as I keep a balanced and healthy diet.

I left London with a lot of shame and guilt that I had allowed all that to happen to me, and I had done the opposite of what I would have loved to express to my loved ones.

On getting back home, now bedridden and not able to get to work, I called in sick after being missing for two days without saying a word. This finally led to the end of my 'Nine to five' office job, which was not one of my greatest joys anyway. I had not previously been able to find the bravery to leave the security of a sure weekly wage, to give myself enough time for my own spiritual development and to face and build a living out of other creative activities I preferred and loved.

But now this event has forced the issue and I have now been sacked from this secured office job, the job I did not have the guts to leave. Now that it happened, I had to make my 'Will' stronger, work on re-aligning and balancing my solar plexus ", the mind of strong decisions" within the center and core of my stomach and being, increasing the power of my belief in myself to effect the change from an office job to my own establishment within my creativity in which I am now successful in, many years after the change.

While at home, the first issue I knew I had to get rid of was the shame and guilt. I apologized and came to terms with those affected. I let the feelings go as I knew very well at this time they were only there for me to show proper remorse towards others affected and now I had to turn towards the positive side of the overall experience.

It led me to the deep realization that whatever will be will be, and truly I did not have to mind what others thought of me as this will never be me but only their perceptions of whatever characters I portrayed for them. I could not continue to seek approval and validation from the outside world as this is an unhealthy practice and would go against the freedom of the self, which was the path that I chose to be on. I do not have to feel responsible towards what others feel for my actions unless it is temporary remorse and understanding, which signifies positively caring for others, so detaching from the negative feelings afterwards was in my own best interest and, in a way, also in theirs. I can not control the feelings of others because this is their own business and responsibility.

You can not go into the heart of someone, knock a few tools around and fix them when it comes to these contexts. This is an impossible task, so the best you can do is prompt and plead for this to happen, as they are the only ones who have the power to allow this and to change themselves regarding how they feel. I can only control my own feelings, and show remorse for them if needed to help harmonise all relationships and also to force the intent of future peaceful actions from myself. There was no point in punishing myself also, holding on to the heavy feelings of guilt as I totally forgave myself for portraying characters I did not like, whether or not others took it upon themselves to forgive me, and most did.

Our physical body is made of eighty percent water, so eating more water based food makes it even easier to keep the body balanced and healthy, which in turn helps to settle the mind. After all, you are, for the most part, what you consume physically and mentally. Therefore, the stomach is the second mind of the body, where your gut feelings are near your abdomen. The spiritualist process calls it the "Solar plexus" chakra or energy point that takes care of the will, self-esteem, decision making and control.

Those who easily get upset stomachs or vomit due to whatever is going on in their surroundings tend to have unbalanced and weaker chakra/energies in the stomach, which in turn affects their decision making and their will. They are very different to those in the opposite spectrum like medical staff who are trained to have very strong stomachs withstanding bloody and gory sights on a day to day basis.

So, the healthier the food you process in your stomach, the stronger and clearer the mind is in the stomach.

Water based food is the most healthy for human physicality, like fruits and vegetables.

There is also other interesting information about the behaviour of water in capturing vibrations which in turn explains the similar characteristics in the human physical machine that is mostly made up of water. There have been numerous scientific studies on ice water crystals and how they turn out to mimic whatever emotions, thoughts, speech or vibrations they are exposed to.

These patterns range from eccentric and beautiful natural designs formed after exposure to 'love, peace or excitement' feelings and energies, in contrast to quite ugly and messy patterns formed from exposure to 'hate, fear or sorrowful' energies, energies which put the body and mind in a dis-eased state. So keeping your vibration, feelings and thoughts in positive states will, in turn, bring you ease and perfect health, while negative states will eventually bring you dis-ease and disease once allowed to fester and manifest in the physical.

(Please see scientific research and experiments done by 'Doctor Masaru Emoto' on "Water Crystals").

This research on the impact of positive and negative energy also signifies the influential propensities we have with one another, that someone smiling can bring a smile to your face or even worse, someone with road rage can introduce that energy to you, and as a defensive reaction or after the driver drives off, you then realize how upset or angry the situation has left you.

The meditational practices I explored within my free time, opened me up to more and other sensitivities towards the benefit of myself and the world around me. I learnt that common oxygen was the key to settling the nerves, and this is the same oxygen found in water, which balances the body, helping to regulate all its functions, as the red blood cells carry the oxygen all over to the places that need it.

I practiced more deep breathing, taking in the oxygen slowly, steadily, comfortably and as long or deep as I could. This I called the breath of life. Then the carbon dioxide is released in the same fashion taking out all impurities and waste products, also escorted out by the stress, tiredness, fatigue and heaviness within, which I called 'death'. This can totally re-balance the nervous system by making the psychological system the mind and the psychological system still and quiet, putting the whole self at ease and with clarity.

In my meditations, I got tuned to more and more of what was within me, from connecting to the broader perspective reasoning flooding the mind through the spirit, to the identification of the lives within me, perpetuated through individual cells or groups of cells within me. I developed a relationship, special bond and communication style with all the cells within me, which brings me back to this dream memory, "The power of the human cells". The cells within us are very powerful, resilient, self-reliant natural powerhouses with the ability to repair themselves and evolve to better capabilities. If taken care of and maintained properly, cells that are old and less active die off while being replaced by new and more evolved ones.

After six years again of no encounter with any sort of sickness or disease, I had just flown back from Nigeria to Ireland with my family, and was ready to fly out again to Spain to celebrate the Christmas and New year of 2019 with the great-grandparents of my son. At this point, my son had brought home a strange and powerful strain of the flu virus which had also infected my wife and mother-in-law. They advised they had already had it for a few days now. We got to Spain and a couple of days into it, I could no longer bear the pain and discomfort my son had to undergo. I was not used to him being drained of energy and not able to play as lively as he would like to, and then his coughing shook my heart so deeply it was unbearable, his fever kept fluctuating.

Up until this point, I had already forgotten how to complain but I found myself automatically complaining to my wife that I did not feel ok and balanced with the situation and urged for him to be taken to the hospital, but my wife assured me that he would eventually be ok.

It was three days until Christmas and we were not in our home country of Ireland. I sensed her expressing a bit of concern about us reaching medical facilities.

I eventually settled myself and strengthened my positivity.

The next day, the twenty-third of December, while looking at my son as I was trying to get him to drink some fruit juice we had sneaked and mixed in with some cough syrup, I decided to perform some sort of energy healing technique whereby everything he had should be transferred to me for him to finally get relief and be completely healed. At this point, I realised that I was deciding to fall sick after all these years of resilience and not taking part in the programming of dis-ease.

And immediately this decision was made, I felt a slight change in my perception and I knew I would come down with this illness too. At this moment, a reasonable and mundane but, according to my perspective, negative thought crept in and whispered that I had just agreed to take in the virus for nothing because it would not concern the speedy recovery of my son.

But I begged to differ and consoled myself that that was not how that healing modality worked and that my world and beliefs were mine, not the beliefs of others. So whatever I believed in that strongly would always work for me, as it was my world to create.

Later that evening, I sensed a tingling but sharp sensation in my throat and I knew the virus had finally arrived. I rushed to my mother-in-law, smiling and advised her that I had now joined them in experiencing this virus. I then asked for the cough medicine to take immediately. I went to my wife and advised the same. I told her I would monitor the whole ordeal and see how my white blood cells tackle the whole thing. I told her that I had the utmost trust in my immune system and the experience should only last three days for the cells to do the majority of their job, and truly this was so.

But it did take my entire body another four days to return to my normal strength and energy.

On the night of that day, as my energies got drained, I felt the onset of a high fever which was a very familiar feeling I used to have while I was growing up in Africa, having been bitten by malaria-infected mosquitoes.

I moved into a foetus position with a smile on my face saying, " hey, old friend, it's been a long time. I almost forgot how you feel".

I drifted in and out of a dream, sometimes being semi-lucid. It was as if I was in a movie theater, watching the cells inside me taking action going from place to place to combat the virus. At some stage, before I woke up, I could vividly see the leader of the cells on some sort of chariot and white horse, leading and shouting out commands to guide the other cells in combating the virus. It was very surreal and looked like some medieval war action movie with beautiful war like creatures from another world. I nodded my head as it seemed like they noticed me watching them, and they went harder as if to show and assure me that all would be taken care of. I woke up narrating the story and describing how they looked to my wife, and it was as if I was looking inside my own body.

I monitored my son as he got a bit better, but I still pressured my wife for us to take him to the hospital, as his cough was still strong and his full strength was not there yet.

We eventually got the appointment for the day after Christmas and at this point, he was already healed and getting stronger as I was also on my way to full recovery. We were one of the first victims of "covid 19" when it started in December 2019. At this stage, the world did not know about the celebrity virus.

One more thing I want to add before I leave this chapter is the importance of the relationship we have with the planet due to our physical apparatus, as a machine, or body of activity and our being in the physical world. Life in this way can not be experienced without it. It is a union we have with mother earth, 'Gaia' as some call it. All that we eat is from parts and elements of the planet that becomes transformed by the powerhouses of our cells into the human physic. A sort of offspring from the human spirit and the planet, a powerful innocent child nonetheless, that should be treated with great care and love. Your body is the temple of God, as they say, and you are the captain to guide and manage it.

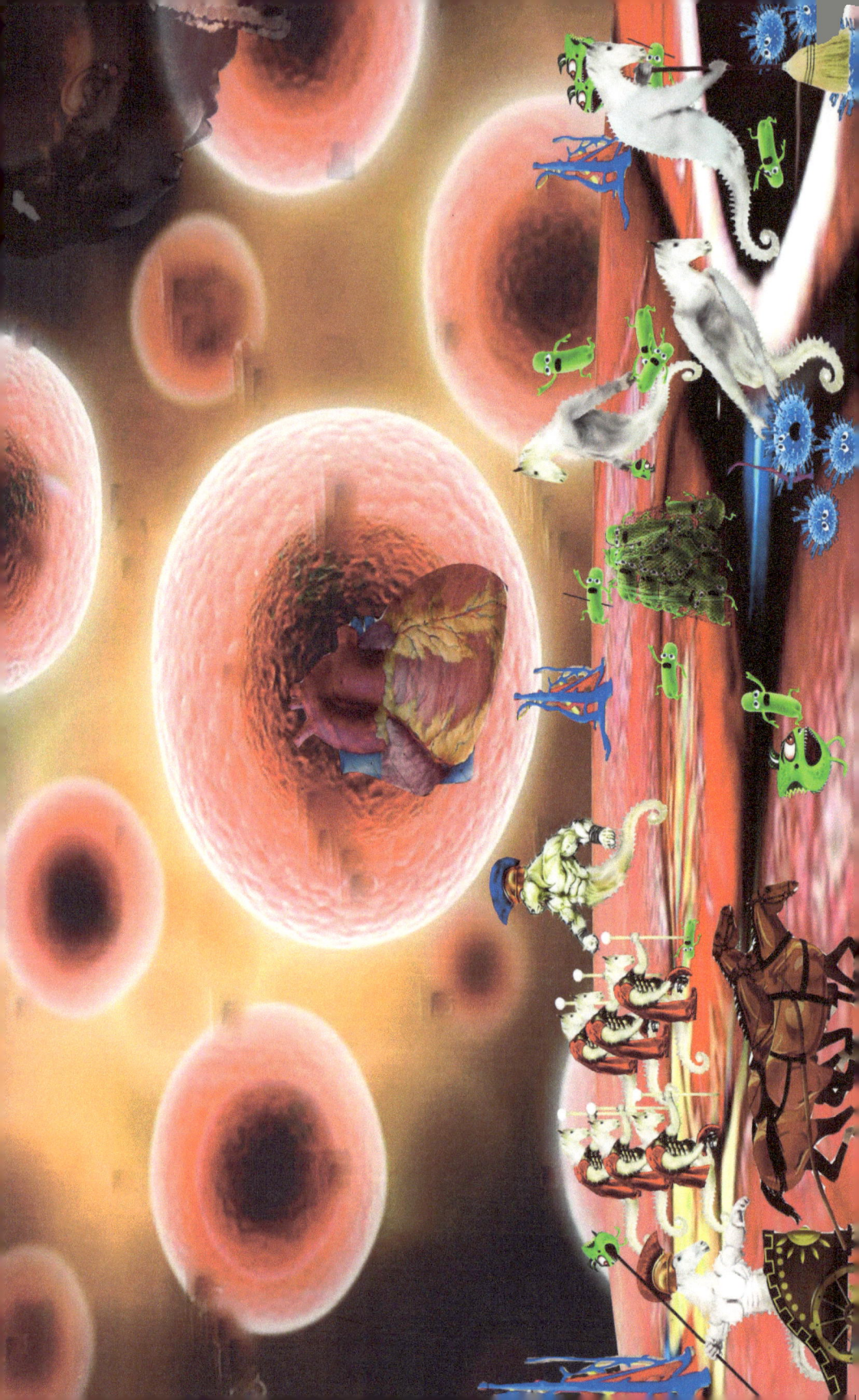

TWENTY-ONE

SELF-SUFFICIENT AND NURTURED

Dream Memories 5th May 2022

In this dream, I remember doing some activities in one of the safest places, if not the safest place, I knew while growing up.

This was my mother's bedroom. Many nights growing up, I would, from time to time, have the luxury of spending the night in my mother's bed.

This felt like heaven and beyond. All my fears and worries seemed to magically disappear as her radiant emanation of love, comfort and assurance gave me the feeling of utmost bliss and tranquillity as I slipped into a peaceful state of deep sleep. I remember my siblings and me fighting to win this grand prize of a position for the night, even up to the point where our own beds and rooms now felt atrocious afterwards.

This tradition was carried on until we each individually outgrew the need for this nurturing and one by one, we crept out of mama's nest to take flight.

In the dream, I was my adult age and alone with one of my cousins doing some work in my mother's room. I seemed to be disgruntled, stressing to my cousin about my unhappiness with something. While I was picking up some papers from the bed, a little candlelight fell on the bed and ignited a small fire. I tried to put it out with my hands or a flickering cloth towel, but it kept coming back alight. I tried putting some water on it but only had a little in the cup. I continued to tell my cousin, who was a bit reluctant at first, that we needed to put this out while I ran to the bathroom to get some water.

Eventually, it went out and then I found myself narrating to other people who magically were now in the room. And as I kept talking, and pointing at the bed, the fire started again and this time, I kept shouting at the people to make sure the fire was put out and not allowed to get worse. They did their best to help but were also quite slow in their reactions. There was also a sense of reluctance in my own behaviour as I was waiting for these people to resolve the matter for me.

I then realised the fire was spreading and these people were incapable of doing the job I relied on them to do. At this point, I dashed to the bathroom to grab a pale of water and poured it on the bed but this was not enough. I ran back to get a bigger bucket but on pouring the water into the room, I could see that the fire had already spread and everyone needed to get out of the house, which eventually got burnt down.

In this dream, I got the inclination that my consciousness was self-encompassing and sufficient to the point that only I knew how to do best whatever it was I needed to do. And if I kept soliciting or delegating these crucial tasks to others, I would only be delaying the inevitable, which could ultimately lead to some type of destruction

The dream transpired into a different location and seemed to be another country in Africa, "South Africa".

In this scenario which was sort of like a club setting, it looked to me as if I was being bullied by some bad boys with weapons.

They were antagonising the group of people I was with. We managed to escape going different ways when I met up with some military men with weapons pointed at me. I was able to talk my way out of the situation, explaining to them that I was innocent and the real culprits were still at large in the club I was running from.

They decided to take me to the club, so I could point them out and for them to apprehend these culprits.

They became quite friendly with me as we went along, but as we got into the lobby of the club, they got quite cozy and comfortable after apprehending the culprits.

It was then one of the people from my group came back in with a vengeance in his eyes to retaliate against the culprits. Seeing me surrounded by these soldiers, he panicked and, in an instant, took all of them out. I was too slow to let him know that these were the wrong guys and, in fact, these guys were only there to help us out.

There was indeed an airy feeling of shock and disgust at this gory sight, coupled with some guilt that was too heavy for me to carry, which immediately put me in a semi-lucid state, whereby I quickly detached from the situation as we walked out of there unharmed and with ease heading to a much safer environment.

This part of the dream showed me more of how I am being taken care of by my higher or inner conscious self, whereby in the face of danger and being within the eye of the storm, I will always manage to get out untouched, as long as I do not stay attached to any fears therein.

And how anything poses any threats towards me, gets taken out even after reconciling with me, as if I am always in a safety net or bubble. I understood and appreciated the innocence of my consciousness and the protection there was for me. This was a teaching I always gave to my son that even as he faced any challenges in life for the purpose of his growth and evolution, he should always know that this will always happen within a safety net of protection that follows him wherever he goes.

I also advise that we should be aware, vigilant and mindful of whatever stories or information we allow to enter our consciousness by paying attention to them, because they tend to become ingredients for whatever experiences we will attract into our lives in the first place.

I remember vividly watching stories of the current war in Ukraine and other gory images from terrorists in Africa, and my dream world then picked from them to use as experience for the purpose of my own growth.

I decided to go into a deep meditation to clear and clean up my consciousness from what I will identify as impurities within my belief system. This would give a reorientation to my mindset and energies in general.

To free the heart space from the psychological grief of negative emotions and feelings, which are only readily available in the lower and much heavier spectrum of vibration and being. Once in the higher, lighter and more positive vibration, the heart space is spared all heavy bombardments of negative thoughts, because only positive and lighter thoughts are readily available at the higher spectrum of being.

This gives the heart space's magnetic force a healthier chance of attracting beneficial ingredients for creation. Your feelings are the key to creating your own reality, so carry an awareness of how you feel at all times, and make sure you are feeling positive so that you can attract the positive.

TWENTY-TWO

TWO DREAMS

Dream Memories 9th May 2022

Part One: (A Rock and a Hard Place)

The first dream I remember on this date, was a kind of repeat situation. Some sort of apocalyptic scenario whereby I found myself between a rock and a hard place.

It was literally a terrain of mountain rocks that led to the ocean. For me, the ocean was a "hard place" because I did not know how to swim. We were running away from some perceived danger that I can not remember, but they were coming from the mountaintop.

The only place for us to hide was a little seashore beach that looked as if, in no time, the tides would come through and engulf the whole land. After going through a miserable feeling of not knowing what to do and thinking long and hard about my options for what were the best chances I had, something in me quickly realised that I had gone through this same situation before and played out all possible actions in different realities whereby in some I survived and some I just simply woke up from. There was no such thing as death as the consciousness just continues to live on, outliving all situations and scenarios as the observer, pure awareness or the one who tells the story afterwards.

It looked like I had found the eternity spot and there was no point or use for fear anymore. I had gone through realities where I hid at the shore and found a safe cave to move into. I had also hidden between the rock and the shore, got engulfed by the sea and found out I could swim or even drown but continued to live underwater as if it did not matter. I became somewhat like a mermaid having an interesting life there and conversing with the fishes. I had floated up somehow and walked on the water, I had jumped on rocks high above the water and found safety somehow. I had even chosen to surrender to my captors and also gone through different types of scenarios and choices with them. It almost looked like the end of the road for this type of trapped feeling, so I chose lucidity to wake up and consciously rewind the times to before I got trapped in the first place and to remember not to take the same path that got me trapped again, because prevention is better than cure and all the drama and interest in such, had been somewhat exhausted in me.

I did not have use for such experiences within my overall consciousness anymore. There was no point in me giving such airtime or attention anymore. I could simply focus on other things to create other realities I was more interested in.

Part Two: (Turn the Other Cheek)

I had been in this dream for a while, but what really stood out for me to reason with and learn from came at the end of it.

I have come a long way in the journey of my evolution since I started writing this book about eight years ago.

Here I am in a house or apartment with many people and many activities going on. At some point, I found myself taking care of a dog that belonged to a friend. The dog was somewhat abandoned by whomsoever my friend left responsible for taking care of it, so I naturally volunteered as there was nobody else left in the house but me and the dog.

I became quite close to the dog in the small space of time and it was as if the dog and I completely understood each other intuitively, our love and bond became strong. I could feel such appreciation and love coming from this pet as it thanked me excitedly, shaking vigorously and moving up and down in the same spot.

I understood his communication to me that I didn't even have to take care of him, as in feeding him and playing with him, but I did anyway! I could see that it was a dog who had experienced a lot of neglect.

I retired to watch some television while sitting on the couch. The dog sat down on the floor beside me and joined me in watching.

Suddenly, he started bending its rear end and proceeded to pass on excrement on the floor right where we were. After a long pause, I intuitively communicated with the dog that that was not a favourable behaviour that humans would tolerate. I stood up, cleaned up the mess and decided to take the dog out for a walk, to see if I could familiarise it with doing such business outside. Then the phone rang, it was my friend, the owner of the dog. I quickly wanted to tell him how I had been the one taking care of his dog, but he stopped me immediately. He commenced to express anger that he had been calling for hours and nobody cared to pick up. He was aware I was in the house and he needed me to do an errand for him around the house.

I advised him that truly I could not see any missed calls and did not hear any rings, but he continued to express his grievances and condemnation of me.

At this point, I understood what was going on and what this lesson was, as this type of experience had happened to me a few times in the awake reality.

I was now a bit semi lucid in this dream as I thought to myself that I would continue my position of love and turn the other cheek as opposed to getting caught up in any arguments, knowing full well that at some point in the future, my friend would realise his mistake and maybe commence to apologise, but for now, I might have to be the one who apologises for what I had not done. Even if he never realises or apologises, he is forgiven anyway! As this is a deep practice and a way to free myself from conflict energies, that are non-beneficial for me as they only serve to weigh me down.

I had trained for this type of thing and had gotten to a point of maturity.

It felt so good to know that this was not my problem and I did not have to hold on to such happenings.

I murmured the words "Jesus Christ" as I smiled with relief and happiness, while my friend kept going at it, slamming and hammering me the best he could on the phone. "Forgive them father for they do not know what they do".

TWENTY-THREE

LUCIDITY IN THE TRUE DREAM STATE

27th May 2022

According to my unique perspective, the true dream state for me is the real world we live in, the one, for the purpose of this book I have called the "Awake Reality".

Now I will share some most recent and real time experiences with you to observe how different dimensions of reality can be simultaneously viewed and understood within us.

Human activities usually start from interests, intentions or desires and are often responses, reactions or retaliations to how these interests or desires are met.

Depending on our belief systems, which are formed from the ways we have been taught or the ways we do things due to the repetition of actions and responses that then form a background programming, it can be easier or harder for us to swiftly maneuver and take future similar actions.

Opportunities pass our way all the time and depending on our various capabilities, we either go for them or not.

I recently got an opportunity to be put forward for a high paying job. This really tested my newly realized belief system that I intend to keep balancing and making steady progress with as I mature.

My belief as a creator that one can create his own reality has been in practice for years, but recently I came across again, one of the teachings I had the privilege to be blessed with about thirteen years ago when I started my journey of self-actualisation.

This teaching, "The power of the I am" by Saint Germain, reminded me of the active, energetic power within the universe that one can align with, experience and regard in all accounts, as when it comes to physical manifestations, materialisations and other sorts of wants and needs, intentions or desires. It strengthened my faith, belief and trust in this and I went head-on and all hands in towards the opportunity.

From time to time, while going through the process of interviews and auditions, I will get tugs from the other side of the coin, my non-beneficial negative beliefs and feelings, trying to pull me in turning the other way, saying I usually would explore these feelings and thoughts by now. Like the "buts" which is like a repetitive psychological program and cycle that we use to trigger and sabotage ourselves. 'You are not strong in that belief so what you want may not happen', or 'Make a plan (B) so you are not all that disappointed', or even the classy 'You are not worthy enough or have not prepared enough, or ready enough, others may be better than you'.

I did my very best not to respond to these urges, except for just saying, 'I give it all to the I AM. This is mine and I made it a mandatory factor for me to feel good afterwards, so I immediately felt the relief of being taken care of.

Finally, the email and phone call came about the job and opportunity, and the agents congratulated me for netting the big job for us all. I smiled with happiness while feeling a bit surprised and not surprised at all. It was as if I knew all I had done correctly for this outcome. I compared it to an older experience whereby I was not so diligent seeing all the actions, engagement and moves that were counterproductive, and there was absolutely nothing else to hide anymore. I could see through the whole process of manifestation, and I murmured to myself that it is true you really reap what you sow.

There was a job I had to work around while going for this new job opportunity with higher pay. I had to organise days off with them due to reorganised appointments and to make myself available for the opportunity. I eventually developed a little resentment towards the organisation but I did my best not to dwell on that, because, on the contrary, the people I dealt with were quite nice and understanding, even supportive.

So why did I still have those feelings? I knew right then and there that that was the illusion, the dimension of lies in comparison to the truth. This is a frequency I am looking to let go of, there was no place for that type of thinking and there was no reason whatsoever to entertain such feelings. These were just resonances of an old self creating a lower self.

I also realised that I felt a little guilty cancelling my day of work with them, and I believe this also added to my state of mind, however, I quickly let this go and moved on to the next thing.

Some days later, after I had enjoyed the opportunity and the high paid job, I got back to my old job with some low energy. My attention did not even go towards doing a pocket sized meditation to boost my energy levels. I just went on in drudgery until I got home.

While I was at home, a feeling and a thought as thick as a dimension made itself known to me. It was the same resentment from the days before, coming through the system to give it another shot, and to see if I really meant it, as I did not purchase what it was selling the first time. It could not fathom why I kindly refused to indulge in its bitter-sweet nectar of suffering. It was quite powerful this time, so I had to play meek and allow it to express all its information and messages, which was, of course, on the complaining side, going through events of the day and just looking for where injustice would have been committed, the fact that I was in low energy made it more powerful increasing its voice.

Since I was quite aware when even in low energy but within an observatory perspective of non-attachment, it felt natural and loving to pay attention and allow this other part of me to express itself fully within me, and for us to have a chance together dispel any untruths. This even increased my energy levels and allowed me to now have a broader perspective from the other side of the coin.

My feelings towards my old job generally changed towards more of a delight and appreciation for the fact that I am on their payroll. Then it hit me 'payroll' as long as I'm on the covid test list, gosh! I had not booked my test yet and it was midnight, a few negative thoughts were trying to invade about how late it was and how I may be stranded, but I neglected them and just went straight to the appreciation that my higher consciousness was trying to remind me all along. But because I was in low energy, therefore in a low vibration, I had to pass through some density and quests before arriving at the realisation of a more direct message. I went online and booked the test with no hassle at all.

The power of holding on to two-dimensional realities simultaneously can allow for the clarity of which one is more beneficial than the other, the one that is more true to you, so to speak, and the one to let go of.

CONCLUSION

Christmas Day 25ᵗʰ December 2019

It is Christmas day as I conclude this long awaited and beautiful book that I started writing approximately six years ago during the Christmas period, after I got fired from my nine to five day job that I had intended to quit but did not have enough bravery, because of the fear of losing the little financial security I had, with receiving weekly wages for almost fourteen years.

I only wanted to concentrate on activities that truly brought me joy and could still provide for me financially. I had been planning how to create more time and space for my career within the entertainment industry and to become an inspirational speaker, which always brought great joy to my heart.

These were my goals up until now and once I left my day job, these things got perfected automatically. It was as if most of my dreams started coming true without the stressful efforts and plans, so before I knew it, I would reach a so-called achievement and say to myself that "was this not what I was dying to achieve years ago? Here it is, but it does not feel anything that special", and this was because my whole mindset had changed and I now knew that I was already everything I was trying to become in the past. Until all my ambitions were dropped and I no longer saw anything as an achievement but instead playful experiences that I enjoyed and passionately took part in from moment to moment.

I was diagnosed with Tuberculosis of the spine in 2009, while on the hospital bed and being poked left, right and centre all over my body and being around the worst of the patients moving in and out of whatever hospitals they had to refer me to. At first, doctors were not even able to tell me what was wrong with me after numerous specialist tests. There was even a time when some student doctors were in my room and there was a lecture going on about my unique case, I felt like a specimen but I do vaguely remember a very kind nurse to whom I gave my consent. I was like half in this world and half in other places of existence that I can not explain. I once made a joke while speaking to my mother on the phone that I was due this holiday and was very glad that I did not have to go back to my nine to five day job just yet. Also, I had a huge screen TV with maids everywhere who brought me food, did everything for me and even went to the toilet for me as I could not leave my bed, so I felt like a wealthy king. She laughed and urged me to eat more because I had significantly dropped in size to the point where one could see my rib cages.

Right before the sickness, I was reaching a pinnacle point in my life where I was about to turn thirty years old. This was a very scary and disappointing period for me because with all the years of hard work and continuous striving, I had still not reached the goals I had set and my loved ones around me. It was compounding and very difficult for me to think that I would become a failure. I became very bitter as I continued to carry on with my day job and concentrate on finishing a nighttime degree course at a university and still have weekend music performances, interviews and the like of that, still pushing my way into the entertainment world, locked up in studios and handling my social media etc. But there was still underneath a positive lining that pushed me to carry on, until one day, on my way to work, I fell down and collapsed next to the Tram railway and then found myself in the hospital.

With all these experiences and after surviving the whole ordeal, I came to the realization that

everything I had been taught since I was born and the direction of my focus, to achieve the dreams and goals set for and before me, was not in the right direction towards realizing what everyone wants at the end of the day, which is Peace, Happiness and Love. I decided to change my entire direction and just find a way to go for Peace, happiness and love without any achievements, which felt to me like cheating life at first, but I was very determined and who said I could not live life in that way? I continued to explore this and then started coming across so many others who have been teaching this same type of way of life I realized had been in existence for thousands of years, and then later started finding out that most of my role models have been hit with and also practicing similar philosophies, as I called it then.

These encouraged me greatly and made me change my direction from concentrating on the outside environment to focusing on the internal environment of my emotional energies within my heart space and belief systems and programming within my mind space that I felt needed to be changed. The theme had now changed to "believing is seeing" as opposed to the old ways of "seeing is believing" that never worked and made me a failure in life.

The song of Micheal Jackson always came to mind that if you want to change the world, you must first change yourself, "Man in the mirror". I commenced and continued my journey towards inner engineering and self-realization until I discovered the powerful tool of our dreams in effecting this evolution.

CONCLUSION

I do hope that I have demonstrated and shown examples of how I have used my dreams to teach myself to change into a new me for the benefit of myself and others around me. The magical evolution of my being.

The dreams have given me the opportunity of a safer environment to extra repetitions of intended conscious choices to reprogram my behavioral patterns lodged within the subconscious mind.

All this practice needs is the awareness of the type of behaviour, which can be deemed as non-beneficial and then the attention to the change, to the new behaviour intended.

The repetitions serve to ensure the change is complete, so the conscious choice of the new behaviour must be constant enough to become the first choice of the subconscious mind in set situations.

Similar to the algorithm on social media, the more active, the more relevance and visibility, and the subconscious will always pick up what's trending.

The subconscious mind sees dreams as another form of reality which invokes set responses and feelings in us that, in turn, feed the subconscious mind regardless of what invoked it. Even daydreaming can provide insight into the subconscious mind, constituting its programmes that we then, in turn, live by on a major basis.

ABOUT THE AUTHOR

While I have been living in Europe for the past twenty-three years, I am of African descent. I have traced my ancestry back to a place called the Agbede Kingdom, which is located within a country now known as Nigeria.

From an early age, I was fascinated by the evolution of humanity. I always kept an open mind for any type of learning I could get, and it did not matter where it came from. I was always keen to seek more knowledge and understanding. I was the type who would rather learn from other people's experiences than go through a hard knock myself. This gave me an edge, but it is true what they say, 'experience is the best teacher', and I too had to go through my own hard knocks to understand the wisdom of this.

It finally happened one day on my way to work, when I collapsed and was rushed to the hospital. After a month or two, having suffered doctors and medical students studying my physical state and doing all sorts of experiments, I was diagnosed with tuberculosis of the spine. The diagnosis rocked me 'mentally' also, so the only thing I could do was to do 'nothing', and just lie there and hope to heal. During my recovery, I felt the only place I could go was up, and

I was starting afresh. I began to see life in a much simpler fashion than I had before; most of my ambitions and plans had faded away and I decided to enjoy and take life one day at a time. This allowed me to explore alternative paths, ones that were beginning to make more sense to me as I was getting back on my feet.

I suddenly began to see clues to all those 'questions without answers'; 'Who we are' 'What we came here for' 'What is the truth?' and 'Am I on the right track?' I drew from within the belief systems I had while growing up, but I also started finding outside support to other things I knew inside of me. This brought me out of my shell and, with more confidence, I began to explore more. I consumed everything from a National Geographic show called *Ancient Aliens* to books like *The Secret* and the *Law of Attraction*. I eventually stumbled upon a wonderful being called Doctor Wayne Dyer, from whom I learnt much. I then moved on to Abraham Hicks, Bashar and many other guides, speakers, channelers and writers.

It was as if I was in a schooling period. When I started researching online, one item of information would lead me to another, mostly specific to whatever I was dealing with or needed at that point in time. I felt I was always being propelled towards the next stage in my own enlightenment.

As I went deeper, it all became lighter and easier. Eventually, before I even opened up my mouth to say I was looking for something, it just showed up at the right time, and, as I continued the practice, it all started making more sense; the right people started showing up at the right moments, everything started becoming more meaningful, right from the simplest things, like looking at a butterfly or giving a mere compliment to someone, to the microscopic thoughts and feelings flowing in the mind and heart.

The Power of Dreams is my first book, and it is the story of my journey.